Editor
Lorin Klistoff, M.A

Managing Editor
Karen J. Goldfluss, M.S. Ed.

Illustrator
Teacher Created Resources Staff

Cover Artist
Brenda DiAntonis

Art Coordinator
Renée Christine Yates

Art Production Manager
Kevin Barnes

Imaging
Rosa C. See

Publisher
Mary D. Smith, M.S. Ed.

DAILY WARM-UPS

Math

GRADE 4

- Over 300 daily math warm-ups
- Includes practice in five key areas:
  - Numbers and Numeration
  - Operations
  - Measurement and Geometry
  - Graphs, Data, and Probability
  - Algebra, Patterns, and Functions
- Ideal for review and test preparation!

Author

Heath Roddy

Teacher Created Resources, Inc.
6421 Industry Way
Westminster, CA 92683
www.teachercreated.com

ISBN: 978-1-4206-3962-9

©2006 Teacher Created Resources, Inc.
Reprinted, 2011
Made in U.S.A.

Table of Contents

Introduction 4

Tracking Sheet 6

Numbers and Numeration 7

Addition 8, 10, 12, 17, 22, 23, 24, 25, 26, 29, 33, 34, 36, 37, 38

Addition (Decimals) 8, 10

Comparing Numbers . . . 12, 14, 15, 18, 36, 38

Decimals 8, 10, 11, 12, 13, 14, 15, 16, 17, 18, 22, 23, 24, 30, 31, 32, 34, 35

Estimation 23, 29, 36

Even/Odd Numbers 8, 15, 35, 37

Expanded Form 16, 21, 28, 28, 29

Fractions 9, 11, 12, 13, 15, 17, 18, 22, 23, 25, 26, 27, 30, 31, 34, 35, 36

Least to Greatest 10, 15, 28, 29, 33

Mixed Numbers 31

Money 12, 15, 19, 21, 32, 34, 38

Multiplication 11, 17, 19, 27

Mystery Number 10, 27, 29, 32, 33

Number Line 9, 13, 18, 26, 34

Percentages 26

Place Value 8, 14, 16, 19, 20, 21, 24, 26, 30, 31, 34, 35, 36

Reading or Writing Numbers/
Number Words 11, 12, 13, 14, 15, 19, 20, 21, 28, 32, 33, 34, 37, 38

Rounding Numbers 22, 28

Standard Form 28

Subtraction 31, 33, 36

Word Problems 10, 11, 12, 13, 14, 15, 17, 19, 21, 22, 23, 24, 25, 26, 27, 29, 30, 31, 32, 33, 34, 36, 37, 38

Answer Key 39

Operations 41

Addition 47, 49, 50, 51, 53, 56, 57, 59, 60, 64, 65, 66, 67, 69, 70, 71, 72

Division 42, 43, 44, 45, 46, 48, 51, 52, 54, 55, 56, 57, 58, 60, 61, 62, 64, 66, 68, 69

Multiplication 43, 44, 45, 47, 48, 49, 50, 51, 52, 53, 54, 55, 57, 58, 59, 60, 61, 63, 64, 65, 67, 68, 69, 70, 71, 72

Reasoning 47, 68

Subtraction 42, 46, 49, 50, 51, 56, 58, 61, 62, 63, 65, 66, 67, 68, 69, 70, 71, 72

Multi-Step Word Problems 42, 43, 44, 45, 46, 48, 49, 50, 51, 52, 53, 56, 57, 59, 61, 62, 63, 64, 65, 66, 67, 68, 69, 70, 71, 72

Vocabulary 63

Answer Key 73

Measurement and Geometry 75

Angles 79, 82, 90, 92, 105

Area 89, 90, 100, 101, 102

Capacity 86, 91, 92, 102

Congruency 76, 78, 83, 96

Converting Measurements 76, 77, 78, 80, 81, 82, 84, 85, 91, 95, 98, 99, 100, 101, 104, 105

Coordinates 93

Edges/Faces/Vertices 77, 88, 89, 90, 91, 94, 104, 105, 106

Estimation 86, 87, 91, 98, 102

Length/Width 78, 84, 94, 101, 102, 103

Line Segments 85, 105

Number Lines 96, 103

Parallel Lines 77, 87, 95, 105

Perimeter 78, 84, 89, 97, 100, 102

Perpendicular Lines 76, 94, 104

Reflection/Rotation/Translation 79, 80, 81, 82, 83, 88, 104

Table of Contents

Symmetry 87, 92, 93

Temperature 83, 97

Three-Dimensional Figures. 77, 79, 86, 88, 89, 90, 91, 93, 94, 100, 104, 106

Two-Dimensional Figures 79, 91, 97, 100 103, 105, 106

Time 80, 83, 87, 90, 96, 98, 100, 101, 106

Vocabulary . . 84, 85, 86, 88, 91, 92, 93, 95, 98

Weight. 87, 95, 96

Word Problems 81, 89, 97, 99

Word Problems (Length) 76, 77, 78, 80, 84, 86, 91, 99, 102, 104

Word Problems (Liquid Measurements) . . . 76, 82, 99

Word Problems (Weight) . . . 77, 81, 85, 96, 98

Answer Key 107

Graphs, Data and Probability 109

Analyzing Data 112, 114, 115, 117, 118, 119, 121, 122, 128, 131, 134, 139

Bar Graphs 114, 115, 116, 117, 120, 124, 125, 128, 129, 130, 132, 137, 138, 139, 140

Combinations 111, 112, 113, 115, 116, 117, 118, 124, 125, 126, 127, 129, 132, 135, 136

Completing Graphs. 125

Median of the Data 115

Order. 128, 131

Patterns 121

Probability Using Cards 130, 134, 135

Probability Using Dice 129, 136, 137

Probability Using Money 110, 113, 136

Probability Using Spinners 111, 112, 113, 114, 117, 120, 121, 122, 123, 125, 126, 127, 130, 132, 133, 136, 138, 139, 140

Reading Graphs 114, 115, 116, 117, 120, 124, 128, 129, 130, 132, 137, 138, 139, 140

Tables. 115, 121, 124, 129, 131, 135, 137, 138

Tally Charts. 125, 128

Unlikely/Likely. 127

Word Problems 110, 111, 112, 113, 114, 115, 116, 117, 118, 119, 120, 122, 123, 124, 125, 128, 130, 131, 134, 140

Answer Key 141

Algebra, Patterns and Functions. 143

Combinations 161

Dot Patterns. 147

Fact Families 163, 165, 166, 174

Functions 145, 146, 148, 151, 153, 154, 159, 161, 163, 164, 166, 174

Letter Patterns. 159, 172

Number Patterns . . 144, 146, 147, 148, 149, 151, 152, 154, 155, 157, 159, 160, 167, 168

Number Sentences 146, 152, 154, 157, 158, 163, 164, 165, 169, 170, 171, 174

Reflection 165

Shape Patterns 145, 147, 150, 161, 162, 164, 165, 167, 173

Solving Equations 148, 149, 150, 156, 157, 159, 160, 162, 163, 164, 165, 166, 169, 170, 171, 172, 173, 174

Time Patterns 149, 151, 153

Reading Tables, Charts, and Graphs. 144, 145, 146, 148, 151, 153, 154, 155, 156, 157, 158, 159, 161, 162, 163, 164, 167, 170, 171, 172, 173, 174

Word Problems 144, 145, 146, 147, 148, 149, 150, 151, 152, 153, 155, 156, 157, 158, 159, 160, 161, 162, 164, 167, 168, 172, 173

Answer Key 175

Introduction

The *Daily Warm-Ups: Math* series was written to provide students with frequent opportunities to master and retain important math skills. The unique format used in this series provides students with the opportunity to improve their own fluency in math. Each section consists of at least 30 pages of challenging problems that meet national and state standards. (See Table of Contents to find a listing of specific subject areas. Answer keys are located at the back of each section.) Use the tracking sheet on page 6 to record which warm-up exercises you have given to your students. Or, distribute copies of the sheet for students to keep their own records.

This book is divided into five sections. The sections are as follows:

- Numbers and Numeration
- Operations
- Measurement and Geometry
- Graphs, Data and Probability
- Algebra, Patterns and Functions

Daily Warm-Ups: Math gives students a year-long collection of challenging problems to reinforce key math skills taught in the classroom. As students become active learners in discovering mathematical relationships, they acquire a necessary understanding that improves their problem-solving skills and, therefore, boosts their confidence in math. When using this book, keep the idea of incorporating the warm-ups with the actual curriculum that you may be currently using in your classroom. This provides students with a greater chance of mastering the math skills.

This book can be used in a variety of ways. However, the exercises in this book were designed to be used as warm-ups where students will have the opportunity to work problems and obtain immediate feedback from their teacher. To help ensure student success, spend a few moments each day discussing problems and solutions. This extra time will not take very long and will yield great results from students! As you use this book, you will be excited to watch your students discover how exciting math concepts can be!

Teaching Tips

Ideas on how to use the warm-ups are as follows:

- *Discussion*—Most warm-ups can be completed in a short amount of time. When time is up, model how to correctly work the problems. You may wish to have students correct their own work. Allow time for students to discuss problems and their solutions to problems. You may want to allow students the opportunity to discuss their answers or the way they solved the problems with partners. Discuss why some answers are correct and why others are not. Students should be able to support their choices. Having students understand that there are many ways of approaching a problem and strategies used in dealing with them are a great benefit for all students. The time you allow students to do this is just as important as the time spent completing the problems.

- *Review*—Give students the warm-up at the end of the lesson as a means of tying in an objective taught that day. The problems students encounter on each warm-up are designed to improve math fluency and are not intended to be included as a math grade. If the student has difficulty with an objective, then review the material again with him or her independently and provide additional instruction.

Teaching Tips *(cont.)*

- *Assessment*—The warm-ups can be used as a preliminary assessment to find out what your students know. Use the assessment to tailor your lessons.

- *Introduction*—Use the warm-ups as an introduction into the new objective to be taught. Select warm-ups according to the specific skill or skills to be introduced. The warm-ups do not have to be distributed in any particular order.

- *Independent Work*—Photocopy the warm-up for students to work on independently.

- *Transparencies*—Make overhead transparencies for each lesson. Present each lesson as a means of introducing an objective not previously taught, or have students work off the transparency.

- *Model*—Invite students to come to the board to model how they approached a problem on the warm-up.

- *Test Preparation*—The warm-ups can be a great way to prepare for math tests in the classroom or for any standardized testing. You may wish to select warm-ups from all sections to use as practice tests and/or review prior to standardized testing.

Student Tips

Below is a chart that you may photocopy and cut out for each student. It will give students a variety of strategies to use when dealing with difficult problems.

Math Tips

✓ Write word problems as number problems.

✓ Underline the question and circle any key words.

✓ Make educated guesses when you encounter multiple-choice problems or problems with which you are not familiar.

✓ Leave harder problems for last. Then, come back to solve those problems after you have completed all other problems on the warm-up.

✓ Use items or problem-solving strategies, such as drawing a diagram or making a table to solve the problem.

✓ Always check your answer to see that it makes sense.

Tracking Sheet

Numbers and Numeration Warm-Ups

1		8		15		22		29		36		43		50		57	
2		9		16		23		30		37		44		51		58	
3		10		17		24		31		38		45		52		59	
4		11		18		25		32		39		46		53		60	
5		12		19		26		33		40		47		54		61	
6		13		20		27		34		41		48		55		62	
7		14		21		28		35		42		49		56			

Operations Warm-Ups

1		8		15		22		29		36		43		50		57	
2		9		16		23		30		37		44		51		58	
3		10		17		24		31		38		45		52		59	
4		11		18		25		32		39		46		53		60	
5		12		19		26		33		40		47		54		61	
6		13		20		27		34		41		48		55		62	
7		14		21		28		35		42		49		56			

Measurement and Geometry Warm-Ups

1		8		15		22		29		36		43		50		57	
2		9		16		23		30		37		44		51		58	
3		10		17		24		31		38		45		52		59	
4		11		18		25		32		39		46		53		60	
5		12		19		26		33		40		47		54		61	
6		13		20		27		34		41		48		55		62	
7		14		21		28		35		42		49		56			

Graphs, Data and Probability Warm-Ups

1		8		15		22		29		36		43		50		57	
2		9		16		23		30		37		44		51		58	
3		10		17		24		31		38		45		52		59	
4		11		18		25		32		39		46		53		60	
5		12		19		26		33		40		47		54		61	
6		13		20		27		34		41		48		55		62	
7		14		21		28		35		42		49		56			

Algebra, Patterns and Functions Warm-Ups

1		8		15		22		29		36		43		50		57	
2		9		16		23		30		37		44		51		58	
3		10		17		24		31		38		45		52		59	
4		11		18		25		32		39		46		53		60	
5		12		19		26		33		40		47		54		61	
6		13		20		27		34		41		48		55		62	
7		14		21		28		35		42		49		56			

NUMBERS AND NUMERATION

DAILY Warm-Up 1

Name _____ Date _____

1. What digit is in the ten thousands place in the number below? *(Circle your answer.)*

4, 8 6 1, 3 9 0

2. What is the largest four-digit even number that can be made with the digits 1, 2, 3, and 4? Each digit can be used only once. *(Write your answer on the line.)*

_____

DAILY Warm-Up 2

Name _____ Date _____

1. Add the decimal number sixteen and nine tenths to twenty-three and seven tenths. *(Show your work. Write your final answer on the line.)*

_____

2. What fraction is shown by the shaded portion of model below? How is this fraction written as a decimal?

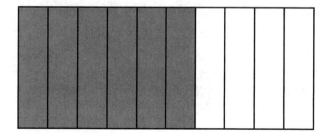

Fraction:_____

Decimal:_____

8

DAILY Warm-Up 3

Name _____ Date _____

1. Circle the letter that represents 2¾ on the number line below.

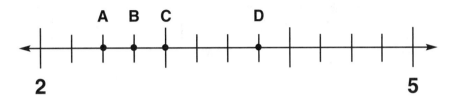

2. Use your pencil to shade in the relationship showing that $\frac{2}{4}$ and $\frac{1}{2}$ are equivalent.

 =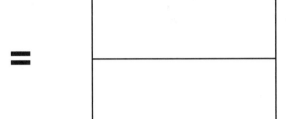

DAILY Warm-Up 4

Name _____ Date _____

1. More than 89,694 fans attended a popular concert. Circle the letter below that shows which could be the number of people who attended.

A. 89,395   **C.** 89,597

B. 89,699   **D.** 89,691

2. Circle the letter of the choice that represents the model shown below.

A. $\frac{12}{3}$ **C.** $\frac{13}{4}$

B. 3   **D.** $3\frac{12}{3}$

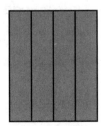  

DAILY
Warm-Up 5

Name _____ Date _____

1. Arrange the decimal numbers below in order from **smallest to largest** on the line below.

| 13.2   1.32   2.13   1.23 |

_____

2. Find the sum when the decimal number fourteen and seven tenths is added to the decimal number four and sixty-seven hundredths. *(Show your work. Write your final answer on the line.)*

_____

DAILY
Warm-Up 6

Name _____ Date _____

1. Can you guess my number? The number is less than 30. The sum of the digits is 10. The number is an even number. What number am I? *(Write your answer on the line.)*

_____

2. Maci is playing a game with her brother Ty. She said she would pick a number and give clues to its identity. Also, for every number Ty guessed right, she would do two sit-ups. The clues she gave are as follows:

- The number is an odd number.
- The sum of the digits is 5.
- The number is less than 25.

What number did Ty guess? _____

How many sit-ups will Maci have to do? _____

Name _____ **Date** _____

1. Margo can jump 58 times in 1 minute. About how many times can Margo jump in 5 minutes? *(Show your work. Write your final answer on the line.)*

_____

2. Write the decimal number that the shaded portion of the model represents on the line.

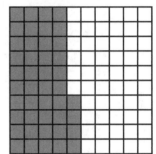

_____

Name _____ **Date** _____

1. Mary and her friends ate $\frac{3}{8}$ of an apple pie that Mary's mom baked. Which model below shows the fraction of the pie left in the unshaded portion? *(Circle the letter for the correct choice.)*

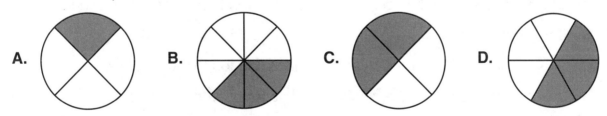

A.   **B.**   **C.**   **D.**

2. At a local charity, one million, three hundred sixty-eight thousand, two hundred eighty-five dollars was raised for cancer research. How is this number written? *(Circle the letter of the correct answer.)*

A. 1,680,285   **B.** 1,860,825   **C.** 1,368,285   **D.** 1,386,285

Name _____   **Date** _____

Warm-Up 9

1. James bought a new computer for $1,200. He also bought a printer for $450. If he wrote a check, for how much did he write the check? *(Circle the letter of the correct answer.)*

   A. One thousand, two hundred dollars

   B. One thousand, four hundred fifty dollars

   C. One thousand, six hundred fifty dollars

   D. Seven hundred fifty dollars

2. Jack walked $\frac{3}{10}$ of a mile on Monday. Which decimal below represents how far Jack walked? *(Circle the letter of the correct answer.)*

   A. 3.0   **B.** 0.3   **C.** 0.03   **D.** Not Given

Name _____   **Date** _____

Warm-Up 10

1. Margo is playing a banking game. She counted all the money and found there was $1,238,450 in play money. How is this number read? *(Circle the letter of the correct answer.)*

   A. One million, two hundred sixty-four thousand, two hundred twelve dollars

   B. One million, two hundred thirty-eight thousand, four hundred fifty dollars

   C. One million, two hundred eighty-three thousand, four hundred fifty dollars

   D. One million, two hundred eight thousand, four hundred fifty dollars

2. Jenny wrote the numbers below on the board. She asked her friend to use comparative symbols to show which number was greater. If her friend answered correctly, which answer identifies her response? *(Circle the letter of the correct answer.)*

   A. 23,456,985 = 23,459,685   **C.** 23,465,585 > 23,985,456

   B. 23,456,985 > 23,654,589   **D.** 23,465,585 < 23,945,654

1. More than 1,500 students attended a dance. Which answer choice below could be the number of students who attended? *(Circle the correct letter.)*

A. 1,239   **B.** 1,697   **C.** 834   **D.** 1,409

2. On the model below, circle the fraction(s) which are equivalent to $\frac{1}{2}$.

1 Whole				
$\frac{1}{2}$			$\frac{1}{2}$	
$\frac{1}{3}$		$\frac{1}{3}$		$\frac{1}{3}$
$\frac{1}{4}$		$\frac{1}{4}$	$\frac{1}{4}$	$\frac{1}{4}$
$\frac{1}{5}$	$\frac{1}{5}$	$\frac{1}{5}$	$\frac{1}{5}$	$\frac{1}{5}$

1. Circle the letter that shows a fraction in the wrong place.

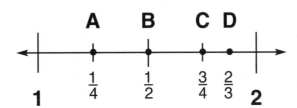

2. Circle the letter by the number that best represents point **W**.

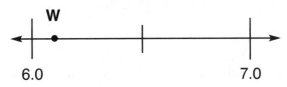

A. 6.0   **B.** 6.2   **C.** 6.5   **D.** 6.9

DAILY
Warm-Up 13

Name _____ **Date** _____

1. Anthony wrote the four numbers below on the board. Circle the letter below which shows a number with a 3 in the thousands place and a 6 in the tens place.

A. 39,463   **B.** 93,462   **C.** 62,493   **D.** 66,932

2. The book Soni is reading has 25,163 words. What is the place value of the digit 2? *(Circle the letter for the correct answer below.)*

A. hundred thousands

B. ten thousands

C. thousands

D. tens

DAILY
Warm-Up 14

Name _____ **Date** _____

1. Mary needs a new car. Her current car has been driven 293,480 miles. Write the number of miles her current car has been driven **in words** in the space below.

_____

_____

_____

2. Which one of the following numbers is **NOT** greater than 3.4? *(Circle the letter for the correct answer.)*

A. three and forty-seven hundredths   **C.** three and thirty-four hundredths

B. three and forty-one hundredths   **D.** three and fifty-seven hundredths

Name _____ **Date** _____

1. Maci is playing a board game with her mother. At the end of the game, Maci had one million, three hundred sixty-four thousand, two hundred six dollars in play money. How is this number written in digits? *(Write your answer on the line.)*

_____

2. Use a comparative symbol to show the relationship of the fraction shown in the shaded model and the decimal number. *(Circle the letter for the correct answer.)*

   A. >

   B. <

   C. =

   D. Not Given

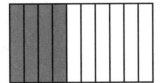 **.5**

Name _____ **Date** _____

1. Lee drew shaded fractions showing their order from **least to greatest**. Which answer choice lists the fractions in order from **least to greatest**? *(Circle the correct letter.)*

   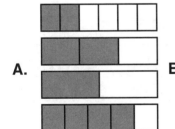 **A.**　　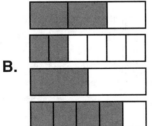 **B.**　　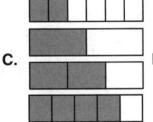 **C.**　　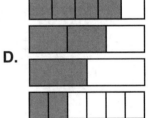 **D.**

2. Miss Pat wrote the numbers 98, 34, 53, 99, 37, and 10 on the board. She asked her students to find which numbers were odd and which numbers were even. Using the chart below, write the correct answers her students gave.

Even	Odd

DAILY
Warm-Up 17

Name _____ Date _____

1. Circle the letter that shows the decimal that represents the shaded portion of the model shown here.

A. 4.6   C. .55

B. .04   D. .46

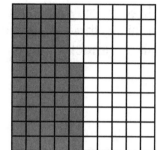

2. Circle the letter that shows 15,294 in expanded form.

A. 100,000 + 5,000 + 200 + 90 + 4   C. 5,000 + 200 + 90 + 4

B. 10,000 + 5,000 + 200 + 90 + 4   D. 10,000 + 200 + 90 + 4

DAILY
Warm-Up 18

Name _____ Date _____

1. Which model below represents 132 correctly? *(Circle the correct letter.)*

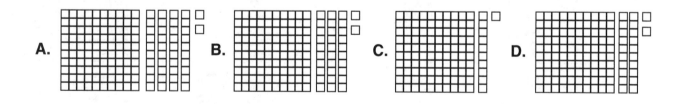

A.   B.   C.   D.

2. Which digit is in the **ten thousands** place in the number 254,136? *(Circle the correct letter.)*

A. 3   B. 4   C. 5   D. 6

Name _____   **Date** _____

Warm-Up 19

1. The shaded model here represents the decimal number 2.27. What fraction shown below represents the decimal number? *(Circle the letter of the correct answer.)*

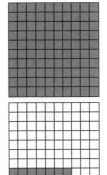
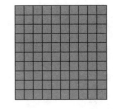

A. $2\frac{27}{100}$ **C.** $2\frac{27}{1000}$

B. $2\frac{37}{100}$ **D.** $2\frac{27}{10}$

2. Shade in 2.54 on the model below. Then write this number as a fraction in the spaces provided.

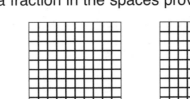

The decimal 2.54 can be written as a fraction.

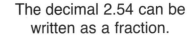

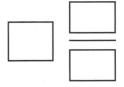

- -

Name _____   **Date** _____

Warm-Up 20

1. While eating at Burger World, Sam counted 12 cars driving into the parking lot in 1 minute. At this rate, how many cars can Sam expect to count in 5 minutes? *(Circle the letter of the best estimate below.)*

A. 20   **B.** 35   **C.** 45   **D.** 60

2. Henry is playing a game at an arcade. If he drops the last two disks, what is the highest score he could make? *(Circle the letter of the correct number below.)*

A. 1,050   **C.** 1,170

B. 1,150   **D.** 1,570

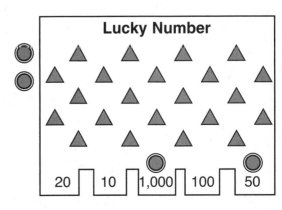

Name _____   **Date** _____

1. The model here is shaded to show $\frac{7}{10}$. On the line, write the decimal below that means the same as that fraction.

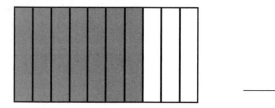

_____

2. What decimal represents the letter **C** on the diagram? *(Circle the letter of the correct answer.)*

   A. .10

   B. .30

   C. .60

   D. .80

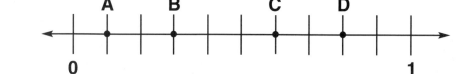

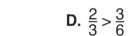

Name _____   **Date** _____

1. Which model below represents one hundred twelve correctly? *(Circle the letter of the correct model.)*

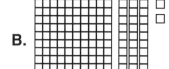 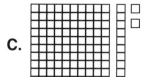 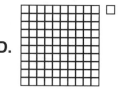

2. Which answer choice shows the relationship of the shaded fractions in the nearby models? *(Circle the correct letter.)*

   A. $\frac{3}{6} > \frac{2}{3}$ **C.** $\frac{2}{3} = \frac{3}{6}$

   B. $\frac{2}{3} < \frac{3}{6}$ **D.** $\frac{2}{3} > \frac{3}{6}$

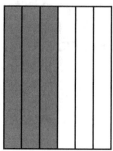 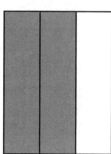

DAILY Warm-Up 23 Name _____ Date _____

1. What does the digit 9 mean in the number 29,458? *(Circle the letter of the correct response below.)*

A. 9 ten thousands

C. 9 hundreds

B. 9 thousands

D. 9 tens

2. Jack bought 3 mini-bikes for his sons. Each bike cost $1,200. If Jack wrote a check for all 3 mini-bikes, for how much money did he write his check? *(Circle the correct letter below.)*

A. three thousand, two hundred dollars

C. two thousand, four hundred dollars

B. one thousand, two hundred dollars

D. three thousand, six hundred dollars

- -

DAILY Warm-Up 24 Name _____ Date _____

1. Yolanda wrote the numbers 127 and 174 on the board. *(Circle the letter of the model that shows these numbers correctly.)*

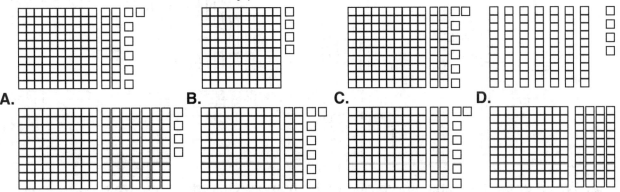

A. **B.** **C.** **D.**

2. Sarah earned 2,345 points playing a board game. Her sister earned 2,349 points playing the same game. Which place value is important in determining who won? *(Circle the letter of the correct answer below.)*

A. ones **B.** tens **C.** hundreds **D.** thousands

Name _____ **Date** _____

DAILY
Warm-Up 25

1. Write out in words what the counting number on the nearby abacus represents.

_____

_____

_____

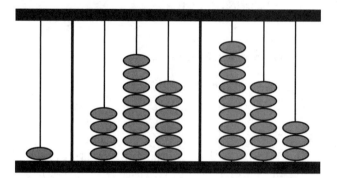

2. Circle the letter below which shows the **largest** number.

A. 38,876   **B.** 36,878   **C.** 36,788   **D.** 38,678

Name _____ **Date** _____

DAILY
Warm-Up 26

1. Circle the letter of the model that shows **more** than two hundred forty-three.

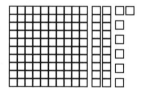
A.

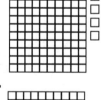
B.

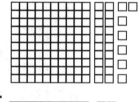
C.

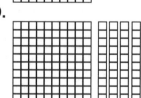
D.

2. Which of the following groups shows the numbers in order from **greatest to least**?
(Circle the letter of the correct response.)

A. 10,234	10,931	10,820	10,452
B. 10,931	10,820	10,452	10,234
C. 10,234	10,452	10,931	10,820
D. 10,234	10,452	10,820	10,931

DAILY
Warm-Up 27

Name _____ Date _____

1. Circle the letter of the answer choice that best represents the number 948.

A. 9 x 10 plus 4 x 10 plus 8 x 1   **C.** 9 x 1000 plus 4 x 100 plus 8 x 1

B. 9 x 100 plus 4 x 10 plus 8 x 1   **D.** 94 x 100 plus 8 x 1

2. Frank bought a new stereo for $246. Write out the amount Frank spent on the check below. *(Use the arrow as your guide.)*

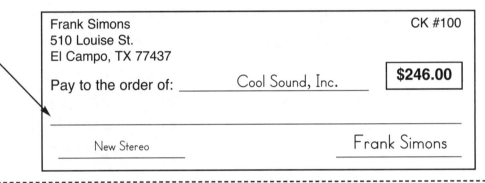

Frank Simons   CK #100
510 Louise St.
El Campo, TX 77437

Pay to the order of: _____ Cool Sound, Inc. _____   **$246.00**

_____

_____ New Stereo _____   Frank Simons

DAILY
Warm-Up 28

Name _____ Date _____

1. Sandra's charity earned $1,230,394 for cancer research. How is this number written in expanded form? *(Circle the letter of the correct response.)*

A. 1,000,000 + 200,000 + 30 + 300 + 90 + 4

B. 1,000,000 + 200,000 + 30,000 + 300 + 90 + 4

C. 100,000 + 2,000 + 300 + 90 + 4

D. 100,000 + 2,000 + 3,000 + 90 + 4

2. David and Heath were playing a video game. When the game finished, David scored 23,456,985 points. Heath scored 23,459,684. What place value is important in determining who won? *(Circle the letter of the correct response.)*

A. tens   **B.** hundreds   **C.** thousands   **D.** ten thousands

DAILY Warm-Up 29

Name _____ Date _____

1. Write the decimal shown on the shaded model below.

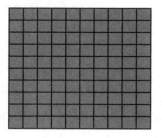 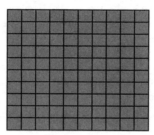 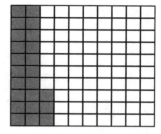 _____

2. The model here is shaded to present the fraction $\frac{7}{10}$. Which answer choice below correctly identifies the fraction **NOT** shaded written as a decimal? *(Circle the letter of the correct answer.)*

A. 7.0   **C.** .30

B. .7   **D.** .03

DAILY Warm-Up 30

Name _____ Date _____

1. Circle the letter of the answer choice below that shows 1,673 rounded to the nearest hundred.

A. 1,650   **B.** 1,700   **C.** 2,000   **D.** 1,670

2. Mrs. Watkins drove 293 miles on Monday, 218 miles on Tuesday, and 179 miles on Wednesday. **About** how many miles did she drive altogether? *(Show your work. Write your final answer on the line.)*

_____

DAILY
Warm-Up 31

Name _____ Date _____

1. Betsy collected cans to recycle. The table below shows the number of cans she turned in during a 4-month period. What is the best estimate of the total number of cans Betsy collected during the 4 months? *(Write your answer on the line. Be sure to round each number to the nearest hundred before finding the total!)*

Cans Recycled	
May	457
June	318
July	572
August	268

_____

2. Circle the letter of the answer that describes the model below.

A. $2\frac{1}{5}$ C. $2\frac{1}{2}$

B. $2\frac{1}{4}$ D. $1\frac{1}{2}$

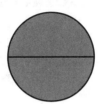 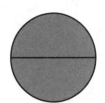 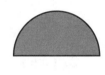

DAILY
Warm-Up 32

Name _____ Date _____

1. With your pencil, shade in the amount that represents 2.04 on the model below.

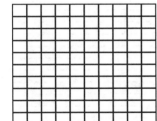 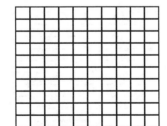 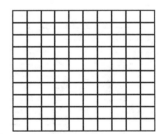

2. Jim is playing a game of cards with his brother. Jim wants to make the smallest number possible with the numbers he drew. If Jim does this correctly, what number would he make? *(Write your answer on the line.)*

_____

DAILY **Warm-Up 33**

Name _____ Date _____

1. When Cindy went to an arcade, there were dart games. She threw 3 darts at each dartboard shown here. Circle the letter that shows Cindy's total score.

A. 126   **C.** 136

B. 16   **D.** 146

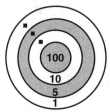 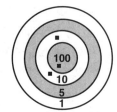

2. Caleb and Angela are playing a board game. Below are the tallied results of the points each had at the end of the game. Circle the letter that shows who won and what the score was.

A. Caleb with 9,451

B. Angela with 4,575

C. Caleb with 5,876

D. Angela with 9,451

Tallied Results of Points Earned Playing Game							
Angela				Caleb			
1,000s	100s	10s	1s	1,000s	100s	10s	1s
IIII	THL	THL II	THL	THL	THL III	THL II	THL I

DAILY **Warm-Up 34**

Name _____ Date _____

1. With your pencil, shade the amount that represents 2.4 on the model below.

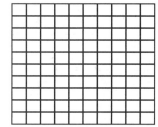 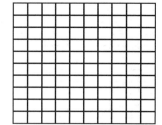 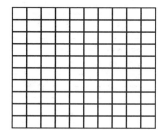

2. Jake is playing horseshoes. After throwing 5 horseshoes, Jake rings 4. Circle the letter that shows how many points Jake scored altogether.

A. 360

B. 260

C. 1600

D. 60

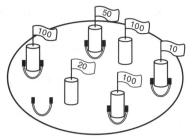

DAILY
Warm-Up 35

Name _____ Date _____

1. Kim's mom bought her a game to play while they drove to her grandmother's house. When Kim shoots the last ball, what is the highest total score she could make? *(Circle the letter of the correct answer.)*

   A. 3,225   **C.** 2,235

   B. 2,335   **D.** 1,000

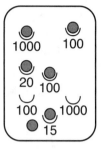

2. Caleb and Angela are playing a board game. How many points altogether did both players earn playing the game? *(Write your final answer on the line.)*

_____

Tallied Results of Points Earned Playing Game							
Angela				Caleb			
1,000s	100s	10s	1s	1,000s	100s	10s	1s
IIII	卌	卌 II	卌 I	卌 I		卌 II	卌 I

DAILY
Warm-Up 36

Name _____ Date _____

1. Pete threw a football 50.3 feet. Cane threw the football 15.45 feet farther than Pete. How far did Cane throw the football? *(Show your work. Write your final answer on the line.)*

_____

2. Maci and her brother Ty baked a pizza their mother had bought. They sliced the pizza into 12 slices. Ty ate 3 slices of the pizza, and Maci ate 2 slices. What fraction of the pizza is left over? *(Write your final answer on the line.)*

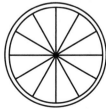

_____

DAILY
Warm-Up 37

1. The shaded area of the drawing below represents the part of Jared's wall that his mom painted. If Jared is going to paint the rest, what percent of the wall does Jared need to paint? *(Circle the letter that shows the correct percentage.)*

A. 15% **C.** 25%

B. 20% **D.** 75%

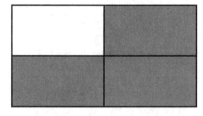

2. Mary swims each day. The number line below represents the times she swam from day to day during a four-day period. How much total time did she swim during the first two days? *(Write your final answer on the line.)*

DAILY
Warm-Up 38

1. Which fraction below represents the shaded amount on the model here? *(Circle the letter of the correct answer.)*

A. $\frac{3}{10}$ **C.** $\frac{7}{10}$

B. $\frac{30}{10}$ **D.** $\frac{3}{100}$

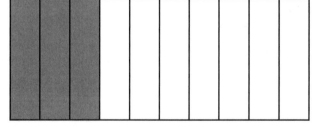

2. Linda wrote the number 1,569,234 on the board. Her teacher asked her how many hundred thousands were in her number. If Linda answered correctly, what answer did she give? *(Write your answer on the line.)*

_____

DAILY Warm-Up 39

Name _____ Date _____

1. A window at Dawson Elementary is made up of 12 panes of glass. While playing kickball, a student accidentally broke 4 of the panes. What fraction of the panes was **NOT** broken? *(Write your answer on the line.)*

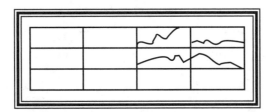

_____

2. Look at the model below. Which fraction below is **equivalent** to the model? *(Circle the letter of the correct answer.)*

A. $\frac{6}{8}$

C. $\frac{1}{3}$

B. $\frac{3}{1}$

D. $\frac{1}{2}$

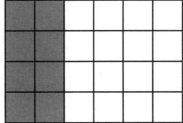

DAILY Warm-Up 40

Name _____ Date _____

1. Jane counted 14 geese in a pond in 1 minute. **About** how many geese could Jane expect to see in 5 minutes? *(Show your work. Write your final answer on the line.)*

_____

2. Can you guess my number? The number is less than 25. The sum of the digits is 7. The number is an even number. What number am I? *(Write your answer on the line.)*

_____

Name _____ **Date** _____

Warm-Up 41

1. **Round** each number to the nearest thousand.

    12,345 _____   38,234 _____   79,124 _____

2. On the line, write the number **two million, five hundred thirty-eight thousand, four hundred seventeen** in standard form.

    _____

- -

Name _____ **Date** _____

Warm-Up 42

1. On the lines, write the number **three hundred sixty-eight thousand, five hundred fifty-three** in expanded form.

    _____

    _____

2. On the lines, put the numbers below in order from **least to greatest**.

    | 64,883 | 65,493 | 46,657 | 64,802 | 64,982 |

    _____   _____   _____   _____   _____

DAILY Warm-Up 43 Name _____ Date _____

1. On Friday, 4,145 people attended the Wharton High School football game. The next Friday, 4,649 people attended the game. Circle the letter below of the best estimate of the total number of people who attended the games.

   A. 1,000   **C.** 11,000

   B. 9,000   **D.** 12,000

2. Cody tells Gordon that he is thinking of a number between 10 and 30. The clues he gave are (a) that the sum of the digits is 9 and (b) that the number is odd. What correct answer did Gordon give? *(Write your answer on the line.)*

   _____

DAILY Warm-Up 44 Name _____ Date _____

1. On the lines, write the number **six hundred eighty-three thousand, five hundred three** in expanded notation.

   _____

   _____

2. On the lines, write the following numbers in order from **least to greatest**.

   | 45,434 | 54,456 | 44,999 | 45,399 |

   _____ _____ _____ _____

DAILY Warm-Up 45

Name _____ Date _____

1. Which decimal below represents the shaded fraction model? *(Circle the letter of the correct answer.)*

A. 4.04   **C.** .4

B. .04   **D.** 1.4

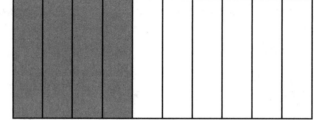

2. Martin wrote a 5-digit number down on paper. He wrote the number 6 in the greatest place value. In the hundreds place, he wrote a 2. He wrote a 9 in the smallest place value. He wrote a 1 in the tens place and an 8 in the thousands place. What number did Martin write? *(Write your answer on the line.)*

_____

DAILY Warm-Up 46

Name _____ Date _____

1. Brenda and Martha ran the 100-yard dash. Martha finished in 45.9 seconds. Brenda's time was 1.23 seconds faster than Martha's. How fast did Brenda run the 100-yard dash? *(Show your work. Write your answer on the line.)*

_____

2. Circle the letter of the answer choice that represents the model.

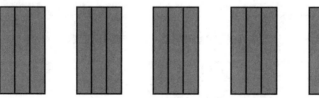

A. $\frac{12}{3}$ **B.** 4   **C.** $\frac{13}{3}$ **D.** $3\frac{1}{3}$

DAILY
Warm-Up 47

Name _____ Date _____

1. Look at the problem below. *(Circle the letter of the correct answer.)*

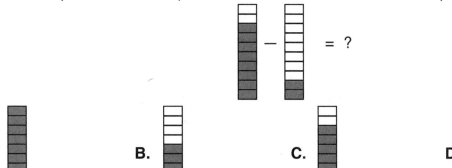

A. **B.** **C.** **D.**

2. Which number below has a 9 in the hundred thousands place and a 3 in the tens place? *(Circle the letter of the correct answer.)*

A. 343,491   **B.** 973,241   **C.** 984,235   **D.** 214,253

DAILY
Warm-Up 48

Name _____ Date _____

1. Mr. McLeary is teaching a lesson on mixed numbers. The model below represents the mixed number he wrote on the board. He asked a student what mixed number the model represents. If the student answered correctly, what was given? *(Circle the letter of the correct answer.)*

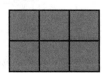 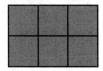 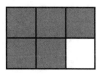

A. $3\frac{4}{6}$ **B.** $2\frac{3}{6}$ **C.** $2\frac{5}{6}$ **D.** $3\frac{3}{6}$

2. What fraction is shown on the shaded area of the model below? How is this fraction written as a decimal?

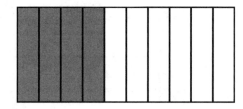

Fraction: _____

Decimal: _____

DAILY
Warm-Up 49

Name _____ Date _____

1. Follow the clues to answer the question.

- I am a 2-digit number.
- I am not inside the trapezoid.
- I am an odd number.
- I am inside the circle and pentagon.
- The sum of my digits is 15.

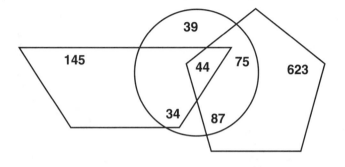

What number am I? _____

2. Solve the problems below. The first two are done for you.

six tenths = _____0.6_____   nine and three tenths = _____9.3_____

eight tenths = _____   five and three tenths = _____

five tenths = _____   eight and eight tenths = _____

two tenths = _____   seven and six tenths = _____

DAILY
Warm-Up 50

Name _____ Date _____

1. Cody emptied his piggy bank so he could buy a new notebook for school. How much money does Cody have to spend? *(Write your answer on the line.)*

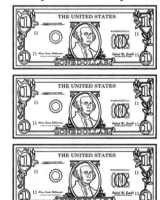

= $ _____

2. How is the number 876,932 written in words? *(Write your answer on the lines.)*

_____

_____

Name _____ **Date** _____

1. The sign below shows the customer count at a popular eating spot. Which customer will be served next? *(Circle the letter of the correct choice.)*

A.)Customer(**229** **C.**)Customer(**230**

B.)Customer(**232** **D.**)Customer(**239**

NOW SERVING
Customer
2 3 1

2. Maci tells Brandi that she is thinking of a number between 10 and 30. The clues she gave are (a) that the sum of the digits is 5 and (b) that the number is even. What correct answer did Brandi give? *(Write your answer on the line.)*

_____

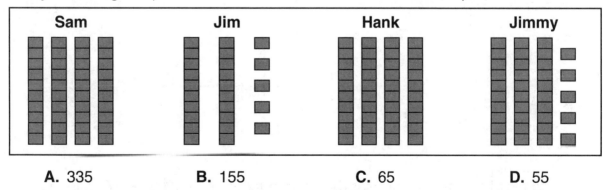

Name _____ **Date** _____

1. Four friends are trying to make a building out of blocks. The pictures below show how many blocks each friend has. If they need a total of 195 blocks, how many more blocks will they need to get? *(Circle the letter of the correct number below.)*

Sam	Jim	Hank	Jimmy

A. 335 **B.** 155 **C.** 65 **D.** 55

2. On the lines, write the numbers below in order of **least to greatest**.

55,434	54,456	54,999	55,399

_____ _____ _____ _____

DAILY
Warm-Up 53

Name _____ Date _____

1. Shane has 10 cubes. The picture shows how many cubes are gray and how many are white. Duane has fewer total cubes than Shane but an equivalent fraction of gray cubes. Circle the letter choice below that shows which group of cubes belongs to Duane.

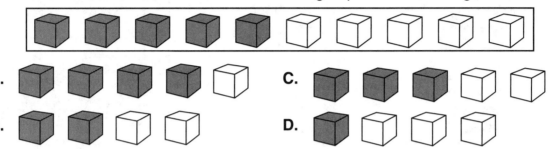

A.   C.

B.   D.

2. Nancy bought two antique chairs that cost $990 each. She also bought an antique desk for $3,500. If she wrote a check, for how much did she write it? *(Circle the letter of the correct choice below.)*

   A. One thousand, nine hundred eighty dollars

   B. Thirty nine thousand, sixty dollars

   C. Three thousand, nine hundred sixty dollars

   D. Not Given

DAILY
Warm-Up 54

Name _____ Date _____

1. Look at the model. Which decimal best represents point **Z**? *(Circle the letter of the correct answer.)*

   A. 2.5

   B. 2.7

   C. 3.6

   D. 2.6

2. Which digit is in the **ten thousands place** in the number 24,319? *(Circle the letter of the correct choice below.)*

   A. 4   **B.** 3   **C.** 2   **D.** 1

DAILY Warm-Up 55   Name _____   Date _____

1. The relationship of $\frac{2}{4} = \frac{1}{2}$ is shown by which answer below? *(Circle the letter of the correct model.)*

A.	B.	C.	D.

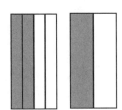 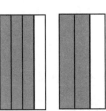 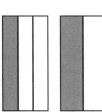 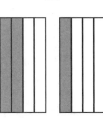

2. Which model below correctly identifies .43? *(Circle the letter of the correct model.)*

A.	B.	C.	D.

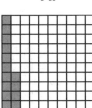 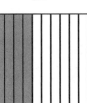 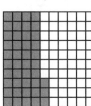 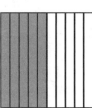

DAILY Warm-Up 56   Name _____   Date _____

1. What is the value of the **underlined** digit? *(Write your answer on the line.)*

$$3, \ \underline{4} \ 9 \ 5, \ 3 \ 4 \ 8$$

_____

2. Circle the shirts that have names with **odd** numbers printed on them.

Name _____ **Date** _____

DAILY Warm-Up 57

1. At Stoneville Elementary, there are 417 students in 4th, 5th, and 6th grades. Today, 197 are on a field trip. What is the best estimate of the number of students still at school? *(Show your work. Write your final answer on the line.)*

_____

2. The table here shows the number of canned goods collected for charity by four students. What is the best estimate of the number of cans collected by all 4 students? *(Write your answer on the line.)*

Student	Cans
Allie	34
Robert	28
Tina	56
Sam	69

_____

Name _____ **Date** _____

DAILY Warm-Up 58

1. Look at the shaded models here. Circle the letter of the response below that shows the correct relationship between the models.

A. $\frac{8}{12} > \frac{7}{8}$ C. $\frac{8}{12} = \frac{7}{8}$

B. $\frac{7}{8} > \frac{8}{12}$ D. $\frac{7}{8} < \frac{8}{12}$

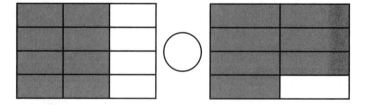

2. What digit is in the **thousands place** in the number 5,129,348? *(Circle the letter of the correct response below.)*

A. 5   B. 1   C. 2   D. 9

DAILY Warm-Up 59

Name _____ Date _____

1. Sarah and Hank wrote the same numbers on the board. The numbers were **8**, **0**, **3**, **1**, and **5**. Hank was supposed to make the greatest number possible while using each number only once. Sarah was supposed to make the smallest number possible while using each number only once. If they both did this correctly, what number did each person make? *(Write your answers in the boxes. You may not use 0 as the first number for this problem.)*

SARAH'S NUMBER	HANK'S NUMBER

2. Brianne is competing with friends to guess the number of jellybeans in a jar. After everyone makes a guess, the teacher says there are **one million, three hundred sixty-four thousand, two hundred six** jellybeans in the jar. How is this written with numbers? *(Write your answer on the line.)*

_____

DAILY Warm-Up 60

Name _____ Date _____

1. A local charity raised one hundred thirty-eight thousand, four hundred ninety-three dollars for cancer research. What would be the amount raised if they had raised ten thousand more dollars than they did? *(Write your answer on the line.)*

$ _____

2. Which of these jars does **NOT** have an even number of marbles? *(Circle the letter for the correct number.)*

A.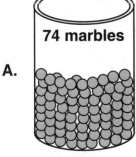
74 marbles

B.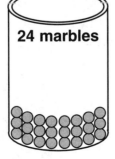
24 marbles

C.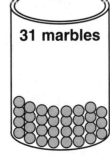
31 marbles

D.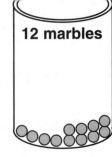
12 marbles

DAILY
Warm-Up 61

Name _____ Date _____

1. Pete bought a car for $23,935. Circle the letter below that shows which check is correctly written by Pete.

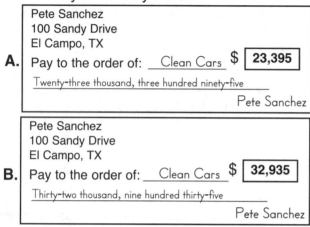

A.
Pete Sanchez
100 Sandy Drive
El Campo, TX
Pay to the order of: __Clean Cars__ $ | **23,395** |
Twenty-three thousand, three hundred ninety-five ____
Pete Sanchez

C.
Pete Sanchez
100 Sandy Drive
El Campo, TX
Pay to the order of: __Clean Cars__ $ | **12,935** |
Twelve thousand, nine hundred thirty-five ____
Pete Sanchez

B.
Pete Sanchez
100 Sandy Drive
El Campo, TX
Pay to the order of: __Clean Cars__ $ | **32,935** |
Thirty-two thousand, nine hundred thirty-five ____
Pete Sanchez

D.
Pete Sanchez
100 Sandy Drive
El Campo, TX
Pay to the order of: __Clean Cars__ $ | **23,935** |
Twenty-three thousand, nine hundred thirty-five ____
Pete Sanchez

2. Peggy spent one hundred twenty-four thousand dollars buying a new house. She spent another thirty-six thousand, nine hundred forty-three dollars on repairs. Circle the letter of the response below that shows how much Peggy spent on her new house altogether.

A. $124,000   **B.** $142,000   **C.** $160,093   **D.** $160,943

- -

DAILY
Warm-Up 62

Name _____ Date _____

1. Teresa sold her cabin for $84,203 dollars. How is this number written? *(Circle the letter of the correct answer.)*

A. Eight hundred and forty thousand, two hundred three dollars

B. Eighty-four million, two hundred three dollars

C. Eighty-four thousand, two hundred three dollars

D. Eighty-four thousand, three hundred two dollars

2. Mr. Bison wrote the numbers below and asked his students to use comparative symbols to find the larger number. If the students answered correctly, which answer did they give? *(Circle the letter of the correct response.)*

A. 4,534,323 (=) 4,934,323   **C.** 4,554,323 (>) 4,564,323

B. 4,535,323 (>) 4,539,323   **D.** 4,534,823 (<) 4,534,923

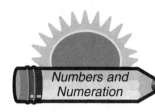

Answer Key

Warm-Up 1
1. The number 6 should be circled.
2. 4,312

Warm-Up 2
1. 40.6
2. 6/10, 0.6

Warm-Up 3
1. The letter B should be circled.
2.

Warm-Up 4
1. B   2. C

Warm-Up 5
1. 1.23, 1.32, 2.13, 13.2
2. 19.37

Warm-Up 6
1. 28
2. 23, 2

Warm-Up 7
1. 290
2. .44

Warm-Up 8
1. B
2. C

Warm-Up 9
1. C
2. B

Warm-Up 10
1. B
2. D

Warm-Up 11
1. B
2. The fraction 1/2 should be circled once and the fractions 1/4 should be circled twice.

Warm-Up 12
1. The letter D should be circled.
2. B

Warm-Up 13
1. B
2. B

Warm-Up 14
1. Two hundred ninety-three thousand, four hundred eighty
2. C

Warm-Up 15
1. 1,364,206
2. B

Warm-Up 16
1. C
2.

Even	Odd
98	53
34	99
10	37

Warm-Up 17
1. D
2. B

Warm-Up 18
1. B
2. C

Warm-Up 19
1. A
2.

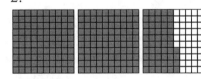

2 54/100

Warm-Up 20
1. D
2. C

Warm-Up 21
1. 0.7 or .7
2. C

Warm-Up 22
1. C
2. D

Warm-Up 23
1. B   2. D

Warm-Up 24
1. A
2. A

Warm-Up 25
1. one million, four hundred eighty-six thousand, nine hundred sixty-three
2. A

Warm-Up 26
1. C
2. B

Warm-Up 27
1. B
2. Two hundred forty-six dollars

Warm-Up 28
1. B
2. C

Warm-Up 29
1. 2.23
2. C

Warm-Up 30
1. B
2. about 700 miles

Warm-Up 31
1. 1,700 cans
2. C

Warm-Up 32
1.

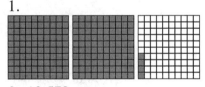

2. 12,579

Warm-Up 33
1. C
2. C

Warm-Up 34
1.

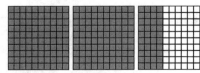

2. B

Answer Key

Warm-Up 35
1. C
2. 10,651

Warm-Up 36
1. 65.75 feet
2. 7/12

Warm-Up 37
1. C
2. 1 hour

Warm-Up 38
1. A
2. 5 hundred thousands

Warm-Up 39
1. 8/12
2. C

Warm-Up 40
1. 75
2. 16

Warm-Up 41
1. 12,000; 38,000; 79,000
2. 2,538,417

Warm-Up 42
1. 300,000 + 60,000 + 8,000 + 500 + 50 + 3
2. 46,657; 64,802; 64,883; 64,982; 65,493

Warm-Up 43
1. B
2. 27

Warm-Up 44
1. 600,000 + 80,000 + 3,000 + 500 + 3
3. 44,999; 45,399; 45,434; 54,456

Warm-Up 45
1. C
2. 68,219

Warm-Up 46
1. 44.67
2. C

Warm-Up 47
1. B
2. C

Warm-Up 48
1. C
2. Fraction: 4/10, Decimal: 0.4

Warm-Up 49
1. 87
2. Column 1: 0.6, 0.8; 0.5; 0.2;
   Column 2: 9.3; 5.3; 8.8; 7.6

Warm-Up 50
1. $5.40
2. Eight hundred seventy-six thousand, nine hundred thirty-two

Warm-Up 51
1. B
2. 14

Warm-Up 52
1. D
2. 54,456; 54,999; 55,399; 55,434

Warm-Up 53
1. B
2. D

Warm-Up 54
1. D
2. C

Warm-Up 55
1. A
2. C

Warm-Up 56
1. 400,000
2. Shirts with the following names should be circled: Beth, Yolanda, and Kathy

Warm-Up 57
1. 200
2. 190

Warm-Up 58
1. B
2. D

Warm-Up 59
1. Sarah = 10,358
   Hank = 85,310
2. 1,364,206

Warm-Up 60
1. 148,493
2. C

Warm-Up 61
1. D
2. D

Warm-Up 62
1. C
2. D

OPERATIONS

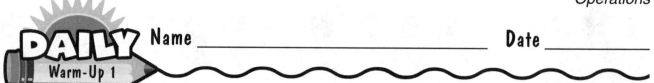

Name _____ **Date** _____

Warm-Up 1

1. Terry needs to buy 46 ice-cream cones for an ice-cream party she is giving her son. Each package of cones costs $3.50 with 7 cones in each package. How many total packages will Terry need to buy in order to have enough cones for the party? *(Show your work. Write your answer on the line.)*

_____

2. What statement about the steps of division is correct? *(Circle the letter of the correct answer.)*

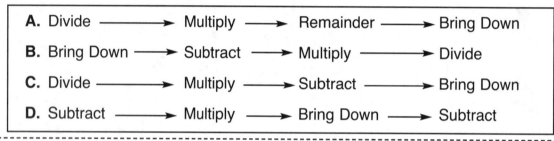

A. Divide ⟶ Multiply ⟶ Remainder ⟶ Bring Down

B. Bring Down ⟶ Subtract ⟶ Multiply ⟶ Divide

C. Divide ⟶ Multiply ⟶ Subtract ⟶ Bring Down

D. Subtract ⟶ Multiply ⟶ Bring Down ⟶ Subtract

Name _____ **Date** _____

Warm-Up 2

1. When you are working a subtraction problem, you are trying to find the . . . *(Circle the letter of the correct answer.)*

A. quotient.   B. difference.   C. sum.   D. product.

2. Mattie worked 12 hours last week. She earns $8 per hour. This week she earned $280. How much money did Mattie earn during both weeks altogether? *(Show your work. Write your final answer on the line.)*

_____

Name _____ **Date** _____

1. Sandra and her sister wanted to take a ride on a sailboat. If both sisters took a turn riding, how many hours were they on the sailboat if they spent a total of $20 altogether? *(Write your answer on the line.)*

Sailboat Ride

$5 per ride,
1 hour,
1 person

_____

2. At a PTA meeting, there were 48 members who showed up for the meeting. There were 6 members in each row. How many rows of seats were there in all? *(Show your work. Write your answer on the line.)*

_____

Name _____ **Date** _____

1. Heath bought grapes at the store. He ate $\frac{1}{2}$ of the grapes himself. His nephew ate 15 grapes watching cartoons. Now there are only 9 grapes left. How many grapes did Heath buy at the store? *(Show your work. Write your answer on the line.)*

_____

2. Which multiplication problem is worked out correctly? *(Circle the letter of the correct answer.)*

A.	B.	C.	D.
3 5	3 5	3 5	3 5
x 5 6	x 5 6	x 5 6	x 5 6
1 8 0	2 1 0	2 3 0	2 1 0
+ 1 7 5 0	+ 2 5 5 0	+ 1 7 5 0	+ 1 7 5 0
1 9 3 0	1 7 6 0	1 9 8 0	1 9 6 0

1. Mrs. Higgs is doing an art project with five students in her class. Each student used a total of 90 sheets of green tissue paper to make the art project. How many total sheets of green tissue paper did the class use? *(Show your work. Write your answer on the line.)*

_____

2. Mr. Watkins has a gasoline can that holds 10 gallons of gas. How many gallons of gasoline are in the tank when the tank is $\frac{1}{2}$ full? *(Show your work. Write your final answer on the line.)*

_____

1. Maggie has 42 pictures she wants to put in a small photo album. Seven pictures can go on each page. How many pages will Maggie use by putting all 42 pictures in the photo album? *(Show your work. Write your answer on the line.)*

_____

2. Mr. Roddy divided 50 pencils equally among 4 students. Twenty of the pencils were red, and the rest were either blue or yellow. Twenty-five of the pencils had green erasers, and the others had red erasers. How many pencils were left over? *(Show your work. Write your answer on the line.)*

_____

Name _____ Date _____

1. Debbie bought 3 small packages of hair ribbons. There were 12 hair ribbons in each package. She also bought 4 large packages of hair ribbons. There were 24 hair ribbons in each large package. How many total hair ribbons did Debbie buy? *(Show your work. Write your final answer on the line.)*

_____

2. Which number is missing from the number sentence below? *(Circle the letter of the correct answer.)*

$$54 \div \boxed{} = 6$$

A. 6   **B.** 7   **C.** 8   **D.** 9

Name _____ Date _____

1. Linda scored 8 goals during a soccer game. Sue scored 2 times as many goals as Linda. Circle the letter below which shows the total number of goals Sue scored.

A. The sum of 8 and 2   **C.** The quotient of 16 and 2

B. The product of 8 and 2   **D.** The difference of 16 and 8

2. Sandra walked for exercise 4 days last week. On Monday, she walked 3 miles. On Tuesday, she walked 5 miles, and on Wednesday she walked 2 miles. Altogether, she walked 15 miles during the 4 days. How many miles did she walk on Thursday? *(Write your final answer on the line.)*

_____

DAILY
Warm-Up 9

Name _____ Date _____

1. Sarah is climbing a mountain that is 1,905 feet high. She has already climbed 489 feet. How many more feet does Sarah still need to climb in order to make it to the top? *(Show your work. Circle the letter of the correct answer below.)*

   A. 2,394 ft.

   B. 1,584 ft.

   C. 1,416 ft.

   D. 584 ft.

2. Lee has 54 tools that he needs to separate into 6 piles. Which type of problem shown below would Lee use to find how many tools need to be in each pile? *(Circle the letter of the correct answer.)*

   A. 54 x 6 =   **B.** 54 ÷ 6 =   **C.** 54 − 6 =   **D.** 54 + 6 =

DAILY
Warm-Up 10

Name _____ Date _____

1. Jennie has 160 stuffed bears in her collection. She is storing her collection of bears in containers that hold 20 stuffed bears. So far, she has already filled 5 containers. How many stuffed bears have **NOT** yet been put in a container for storage? *(Show your work. Write your final answer on the line.)*

   _____

2. There were 76 birds on the playground at Dawson Elementary. Later, 58 birds flew away. Ten minutes later, another 19 joined the remaining birds. How many birds are now on the playground? *(Show your work. Write your final answer on the line.)*

   _____

DAILY
Warm-Up 11

Name _____   Date _____

1. Which expression below does **NOT** have a sum of 84? *(Circle the letter of the correct expression.)*

   A. 62 + 22   **B.** 54 + 30   **C.** 45 + 39   **D.** 34 + 15

2. Gordon has 5 DVD movies per shelf on 6 different shelves in his living room. Circle the letter for the choice below that will correctly show how many total DVD's Gordon has.

   A. The sum of 5 and 6

   B. The product of 5 and 6

   C. The quotient of 6 and 5

   D. The difference of 6 and 5

DAILY
Warm-Up 12

Name _____   Date _____

1. Farmer Leroy plants tomatoes each year. This year he planted 14 rows of tomatoes. There were 28 tomato plants in each row. How many total tomato plants did Farmer Leroy plant? *(Show your work. Write your final answer on the line.)*

   _____

2. Alicia made a pattern of stars. Look at the number sentences. Which one **CANNOT** be used to find the total number of stars? *(Circle the correct letter below.)*

   A. 6 + 6 + 6 = ?

   B. 6 x 3 = ?

   C. 3 x 5 = ?

   D. 3 + 3 + 3 + 3 + 3 + 3 = ?

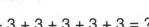

Name _____ **Date** _____

1. Cody has 45 baseball cards. He divided the cards into 9 different stacks. Which answer choice shows the total number of cards there were in each stack? *(Circle the letter of the correct answer.)*

   A. The sum of 45 and 9   **C.** The quotient of 45 and 9

   B. The product of 45 and 9   **D.** The difference of 45 and 9

2. Marty bought candy bars for 3 dozen children. The candy bars come in boxes containing 12 bars. How many boxes of candy bars did Marty buy in order for all children to receive exactly 1 candy bar? *(Show your work. Circle the letter of the correct answer.)*

   A. 1
   B. 2
   C. 3
   D. 4

Name _____ **Date** _____

1. A group of 50 family members took cars to the Rose family reunion. If 6 people could ride in 1 car, how many total cars were needed for all 50 family members to attend? *(Show your work. Write your final answer on the line.)*

   _____

2. Wanda bought 3 boxes of candy for $3 each and 4 hairbrushes that were priced at 2 for $4. Three of the hairbrushes were green and the rest were black. How much money did Wanda spend altogether? *(Show your work. Write your final answer on the line.)*

_____

DAILY
Warm-Up 15

Name _____ Date _____

1. At a fundraiser, 538 bags of popcorn were sold during the morning sale. That afternoon, 349 bags of popcorn were sold. How many total bags of popcorn were sold during the day? (*Show your work. Write your final answer on the line.*)

_____

2. Tracy bought oranges that were priced at 2 oranges for 16 cents. If she bought 8 oranges, what was the total amount of money that Tracey spent on oranges? (*Show your work. Write your final answer on the line.*)

_____

DAILY
Warm-Up 16

Name _____ Date _____

1. Sandra agreed to buy a used car for $3,600. A payment of $1,900 was made as a down payment. How much money does Sandra still owe? (*Show your work. Write your final answer on the line.*)

_____

2. The Barley family is on the way to their grandmother's house. Their grandmother lives 335 miles away. So far, they have traveled 159 miles. How many more miles do they need to travel? (*Show your work. Write your final answer on the line.*)

_____

Name _____ **Date** _____

Warm-Up 17

1. Greg is saving to go on a trip to Europe. He needs $1,090 for the trip. He has saved $250 tutoring after school, $90 for mowing lawns, and $180 for his garage sale. How much more money does Greg need to save in order to go on his trip? (*Show your work. Write your final answer on the line.*)

_____

2. Sue bought 3 packages of buttons. Each package contained 129 buttons. How many total buttons did the 3 packages of buttons contain? (*Show your work. Circle the letter of the correct answer below.*)

A. 387 buttons

B. 132 buttons

C. 126 buttons

D. 43 buttons

Name _____ **Date** _____

Warm-Up 18

1. On Christmas Eve, it snowed. Heath made a snowman in his front yard. It took 10 buckets of snow to make the bottom part of the snowman, 8 buckets of snow to make the middle, and 4 buckets of snow to make the head. How many total buckets of snow did it take to make the snowman? (*Show your work. Write your final answer on the line.*)

_____

2. Mr. Watkins sold cars during the summer. During the month of May, he sold 98 cars. During June, he sold 114 cars. At the beginning of July, there were only 76 cars left on the lot. How many total cars did Mr. Watkins sell during the months of May and June? (*Show your work. Write your final answer on the line.*)

_____

DAILY Warm-Up 19   Name _____   Date _____

1. Logan bought 2 shirts that cost $15 each. He also bought 3 packages of socks that cost $6 for each package. Circle the letter of the number sentence that shows how to find how much money Logan spent.

    A. 3 x 2 + 15

    B. 2 x 15 + 3

    C. 2 x 15 + 6

    D. 2 x 15 + 3 x 6

2. For each "A" Pete earns, his father gives him $10. For each "B" Pete earns, his father gives him $5. Pete has already earned 4 "A's" and 3 "B's." In the space below, write the equation to illustrate the money he received for each "A" and "B." Write the total amount he received on the line to the right.

Total Amount Received: _____

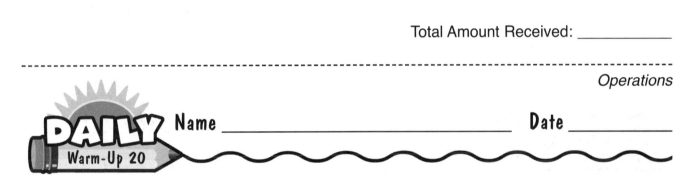

DAILY Warm-Up 20   Name _____   Date _____

1. Mattie bought 2 dozen cookies for his class party. Every student, including Mattie, ate 1 cookie. When Mattie looked in the box, there were only 3 cookies left. If only students in Mattie's class ate the cookies, how many students were in Mattie's class? (*Show your work. Write your final answer on the line.*)

_____

2. Mark is an artist. He paints 6 pictures each day. Each picture sells for $25. Circle the letter for the expression that shows how to find the amount of money Mark earns in 1 week (7 days).

    A. 6 x 25

    B. 6 x 7 + 25

    C. 6 x 25 x 7

    D. 25 x 7 + 6

Name _____ Date _____

1. Into how many groups of 5 can the stars shown here be divided? (*Circle the letter of the correct answer.*)

   A. 2 with 5 left over

   B. 3 with 3 left over

   C. 4 with 2 left over

   D. 5 with 3 left over

2. Kane bought 3 boxes of candy. There were 12 candy bars in each box. Four of the candy bars had peanuts, and the rest had caramel. Each box cost $4.90. How many candy bars did Kane buy? (*Show your work. Write your final answer on the line.*)

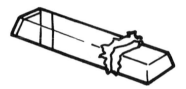

_____

Name _____ Date _____

1. Lois charges $25 for each yard she mows. Over the summer, she mowed 63 yards. How much money did Lois earn? (*Show your work. Write your final answer on the line.*)

_____

2. Justin bought 8 cases of soda for his sister's party. There were 24 cans in each case. How many cans of soda did Justin buy altogether? (*Show your work. Write your final answer on the line.*)

_____

Name _____ **Date** _____

1. James spent $45 on new shoes, $38 on a new shirt, and $32 on a new pair of jeans. He left the store but went back and bought another new pair of jeans. How much money did James spend altogether? (*Show your work. Write your final answer on the line.*)

_____

2. Mark bought 9 cases of grape soda. Each case held 24 cans. He also bought 6 cases of orange soda. Each case also held 24 cans. How many total orange and grape sodas did Mark purchase? (*Show your work. Write your final answer on the line.*)

_____

Name _____ **Date** _____

1. Which pair of numbers best completes the equation? (*Circle the letter of the correct answer.*)

$$\boxed{} \times 100 = \bigcirc$$

A. 65 and 650   C. 605 and 6050

B. 65 and 6500   D. 650 and 6500

2. At Drew Elementary, there are 15 classrooms with 30 students in each room. Circle the letter for the correct number sentence to show the total number of students in the school.

A. 30 + 15 =   **B.** 30 − 15 =   **C.** 30 x 15 =   **D.** 30 x 30 =

DAILY **Warm-Up 25**

Name _____ Date _____

1. Look at the array of faces shown. What multiplication number sentence does the array show? (*Circle the correct letter.*)

A. 4 x 8 = 32

B. 8 + 4 = 12

C. 8 − 4 = 4

D. 32 x 4 = 128

2. Wanda has 64 buttons. She plans to use an equal number on each of the eight shirts she is sewing for her son. Circle the letter choice below that shows how to find how many buttons Wanda will use on each shirt.

A. 64 + 8 =   **B.** 64 ÷ 8 =   **C.** 64 x 8 =   **D.** 64 − 8 =

DAILY **Warm-Up 26**

Name _____ Date _____

1. Write the number that is missing in the number sentence below.

$$42 \div \underline{\hspace{2cm}} = 6$$

2. Terri made an octagon for her mother. On each side of the octagon, Terri used 3 different colors to draw a picture. How many total colors did Terri use coloring the octagon? (*Circle the correct letter choice below.*)

A. 3

B. 8

C. 5

D. 24

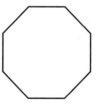

1. Louise has a photo album. Six pictures will fit on one page. There are 54 pages in the album. How many photos can Louise put in the album? (*Show your work. Write your final answer on the line.*)

_____

2. Wanda is making 2 sandwiches for each of her 6 children. On each sandwich, Wanda places 2 pieces of cheese. Wanda looks in the refrigerator and finds 28 pieces of cheese. How many pieces of cheese will Wanda have left after making her children's sandwiches? (*Show your work. Circle the letter of the correct answer below.*)

A. 2

B. 3

C. 4

D. 5

1. Solve the division problem to find the unknown quotient. *(Fill in the boxes.)*

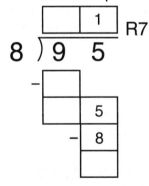

2. Michael has 75 sweaters that he wants to separate equally into 5 different containers for storage. How many sweaters will Michael put into each container? (*Show your work. Write your final answer on the line.*)

_____

55

Name _____   **Date** _____

1. Dawson Elementary is having a bake sale to raise money for a children's author to visit the school library. At the bake sale, Mrs. Watkins brought 12 cupcakes. Half of the cupcakes have chocolate frosting. A quarter of the cupcakes have vanilla frosting, and the rest have strawberry frosting. How many cupcakes have strawberry frosting? (*Circle the letter of the correct answer below.*)

A. 5

B. 4

C. 3

D. 2

2. The Rodriguez family drove 858 miles on the first day of their vacation. They drove 498 miles on the second day. How many miles did they drive during both days? (*Show your work. Write your final answer on the line.*)

_____

- -

Name _____   **Date** _____

1. The new TV Maria wants costs $384.84. She knows she will also have to pay $15.45 in taxes. She has saved $254 already. How much money does Maria still need to save in order to purchase the TV? (*Show your work. Write your final answer on the line.*)

_____

2. Terry is making cakes with strawberry topping. She has 39 strawberries that she wants to place equally among 5 cakes. If she does this correctly, how many strawberries will Terry have left? (*Circle the letter of the correct answer.*)

A. 2   **B.** 3   **C.** 4   **D.** 5

DAILY Name _____ Date _____
Warm-Up 31

1. Elton has a collection of 147 baseball cards. He wants to place them in an album with 7 baseball cards on each page. What could Elton do to find how many pages he will need for his album? (*Circle the letter for the correct choice below.*)

    A. Subtract 7 from 147   **C.** Multiply 147 by 7

    B. Add 147 and 7   **D.** Divide 147 by 7

2. Sam is entered in a hotdog-eating contest. Sam ate a total of 13 hotdogs. He ate 2 hotdogs every 4 minutes. How many minutes did it take Sam to eat all 13 hotdogs? (*Show your work. Write your final answer on the line.*)

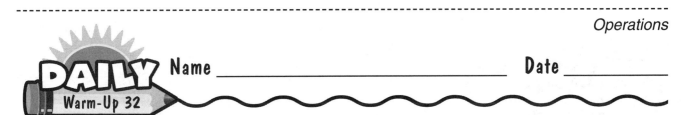

_____

DAILY Name _____ Date _____
Warm-Up 32

1. Abby bought flowers like the ones below to plant in her yard. Divide the flowers into groups of 9.

How many groups of 9 are there? _____

How many flowers are left over? _____

2. Mrs. Watkins went shopping and bought a comforter for $89 and a set of curtains for $64. She also bought a set of dishes for $49. How much did she pay for all the items? (*Show your work. Write your final answer on the line.*)

_____

DAILY Warm-Up 33

Name _____   Date _____

1. Curtis took 48 pictures while on vacation. When he had the pictures developed, he found half of the pictures were overexposed. How many pictures were overexposed? (*Show your work. Write your final answer on the line.*)

_____

2. Mark bought 19 baseball cards from his friend. Mark now has 150 baseball cards. Lou has 24 more baseball cards than Mark. How many baseball cards did Mark have before he bought any cards from his friend? (*Show your work. Write your final answer on the line.*)

_____

DAILY Warm-Up 34

Name _____   Date _____

1. What is the product of 12 and 7? (*Show your work. Write your final answer on the line.*)

_____

2. In Mrs. Schumann's office building, there are 12 floors with 47 offices on each floor. Circle the letter of the correct number sentence below to show the total number of offices in the building.

A. 47 + 12 =   **B.** 47 − 12 =   **C.** 47 x 12 =   **D.** 47 x 47 =

DAILY Name _____ Date _____

Warm-Up 35

1. Sandra's flower mart has 217 vases. If she places 7 flowers in each vase, how many flowers will she need? (*Show your work. Write your final answer on the line.*)

_____

2. Sue has pictures of her grandchildren on shelves in her living room. She has 15 pictures on the top shelf. She has twice as many pictures on each of the next 2 shelves. On the last shelf, she has 6 more pictures than she does on the top shelf. Circle the expression below which shows how to find the total number of pictures Sue has on all 4 shelves.

A. 15 x 3 =

C. 15 + 60 + 21 =

B. 15 + 30 + 30 =

D. 15 x 2 + 21=

DAILY Name _____ Date _____

Warm-Up 36

1. Hank bought 2 shirts for $8 each and 4 new hats that cost $12 each. Circle the letter of the number sentence below that can be used to find the total amount of money that Hank spent.

A. $8 x $4 = ☐   **B.** $16 + $48 = ☐   **C.** $12 + $8 = ☐   **D.** $16 + $12 = ☐

2. Cindy bought 9 cases of oil for her father's gas station. There were 24 cans of oil in each case. How many cans of oil did Cindy buy altogether? (*Show your work. Write your final answer on the line.*)

_____

DAILY Warm-Up 37 Name _____ Date _____

1. Carmen picked 16 tomatoes from her garden on Monday, 18 tomatoes on Tuesday, and 23 tomatoes on Wednesday. On Thursday, she didn't pick any tomatoes. On Friday, she picked 12 more than she did on Monday. How many tomatoes did Carmen pick altogether? (*Show your work. Write your final answer on the line.*)

_____

2. David has 12 video games. Leon has 3 times as many video games as David. Which choice below shows the total number of video games Leon has? (*Circle the letter of the correct choice.*)

A. The sum of 12 and 3   **C.** The quotient of 12 and 3

B. The product of 12 and 3   **D.** The difference of 12 and 3

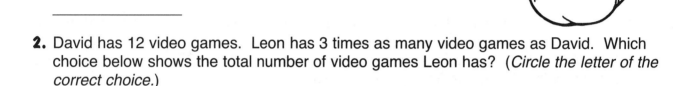

DAILY Warm-Up 38 Name _____ Date _____

1. Joy has 6 hair ribbons. Presley has twice as many hair ribbons as Joy. What should you do to find the total number of hair ribbons that Presley has?

Explain:_____

_____

_____

2. Circle the letter for the correct solution for the problem below.

A. 7

B. 8

C. 9

D. Not Given

$$72 \div \boxed{} = 8$$

![Daily Warm-Up 39]

Name _____ **Date** _____

1. Four friends picked apples at an orchard. The baskets below show how many each friend picked. If they plan to share all the apples equally, how many apples will each friend get? (*Write your answer on the line.*)

_____

Gordon
13 apples

Brandi
33 apples

Cody
53 apples

Maci
25 apples

2. Circle the letter for the number sentence that will give a product of 18.

A. 6 ÷ 3 =   **B.** 6 x 3 =   **C.** 6 − 3 =   **D.** 6 + 3 =

![Daily Warm-Up 40]

Name _____ **Date** _____

1. Emma bought six 12-packs of soda. The total cost of the sodas was $18. Which of the following number sentences can be used to determine the correct cost of one 12-pack of soda? (*Circle the correct letter for your answer.*)

A. $18 − 6 = ☐   **B.** $18 + 6 = ☐   **C.** $18 − 6 = ☐   **D.** $18 ÷ 6 = ☐

2. The chart here shows the amount of money raised for cancer research during different years. How much more money was raised in 2002 than in 2000? (*Circle the letter for the correct answer.*)

A. 1 million   **C.** 10 million

B. 4 million   **D.** 12 million

Money Raised for Cancer Research	
1999	2 million
2000	3 million
2001	5 million
2002	7 million

DAILY Warm-Up 41   Name _____   Date _____

1. Robin works at the post office. She has 144 letters she needs to place in 12 different containers. If she places an equal number of letters in each container, how many letters will there be in each container? (*Show your work. Write your final answer on the line.*)

_____

2. Mrs. Hinojosa has 168 buttons. She uses $\frac{1}{2}$ of the buttons on an art project with her class. She then gives $\frac{1}{2}$ of the remaining buttons to another teacher. How many buttons does Mrs. Hinojosa have left? (*Show your work. Write your final answer on the line.*)

_____

DAILY Warm-Up 42   Name _____   Date _____

1. Lou has 35 markers. He plans to share them equally among 4 other friends and himself. How many total markers will each person get? (*Show your work. Write your final answer on the line.*)

_____

2. Brad bought 3 items at the store. He spent a total of $85. The first item cost $35. The second item he bought cost $20. How much did Brad spend on the third item? (*Show your work. Write your final answer on the line.*)

_____

Name _____ **Date** _____

Warm-Up 43

1. Sloane wants to purchase a 27" TV. At Kalinowski TV Center, 27" TVs cost $590. The same TV costs $495 at Martin Electronics. How much money will Sloane save if she buys her TV at Martin Electronics rather than at Kalinowski TV Center? (*Show your work. Write your final answer on the line.*)

_____

2. Match each word on the left with the letter of the correct answer choice on the right.

    1. Quotient _____   **A.** Add

    2. Product _____   **B.** Subtract

    3. Difference _____   **C.** Divide

    4. Sum _____   **D.** Multiply

Name _____ **Date** _____

Warm-Up 44

1. Seth bought 10 cases of soda that were priced at 2 for $5. How much money did Seth spend on the soda? (*Show your work. Write your final answer on the line.*)

_____

2. Thomas is counting the 1st, 2nd, and 3rd place ribbons he won in track. Thomas placed the ribbons in groups of 8. Which number sentence shows the number of ribbons Thomas has in all? (*Circle the letter of the correct answer.*)

A. 4 + 8 = 12

B. 8 − 4 = 4

C. 8 x 4 = 32

D. 32 − 4 = 28

DAILY
Warm-Up 45

Name _____   **Date** _____

1. Cody bought 4 packages of guitar strings that cost $3 for each package. She also found guitar picks on sale at 2 for 46 cents. Cody decided to buy 7 guitar picks. How much money did Cody spend altogether? (*Show your work. Write your final answer on the line.*)

_____

2. Larry likes tomato soup. The 12-ounce cans are priced at 2 for $1.50. The 8-ounce cans are priced at 2 for $1.00. If Larry purchased 3 twelve-ounce cans and 6 eight-ounce cans, how much money did Larry spend? (*Show your work. Write your final answer on the line.*)

_____

DAILY
Warm-Up 46

Name _____   **Date** _____

1. Walt earns $5 for each dog he walks. On Monday, he walked 12 dogs. On Tuesday, he walked 9 dogs. On Wednesday, he walked 4 dogs. On Thursday, he walked twice as many as he did on Monday. How much money altogether did Walt earn on Monday, Tuesday, Wednesday, and Thursday walking dogs? (*Show your work. Write your final answer on the line.*)

_____

2. Kerry and David own a racing car together. If they sell the car for $9,500, how much money will each person get? (*Show your work. Write your final answer on the line.*)

_____

1. Jennifer needed paper clips for her new job. She purchased 3 packages of large paper clips that had 245 paper clips in each package. She also bought 4 packages of small paper clips that had 280 paper clips in each package. How many paper clips does Jennifer have altogether? (*Show your work. Write your final answer on the line.*)

_____

2. The sunflower bus that left Dawson Elementary has 25 more passengers than the football bus. The sunflower bus has 90 passengers. Which of the choices below can be used to find how many passengers are on the football bus? (*Circle the correct letter.*)

A. The sum of 90 and 12

B. The product of 90 and 5

C. The difference between 90 and 25

D. The difference between 25 and 12

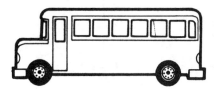

---

1. Jack is buying 20 music CDs. He buys 8 rock CDs, 5 rap CDs, and the rest are country CDs. Which of the following choices shows how to find the number of country CDs Jack bought? (*Circle the correct letter.*)

A. Add 8 and 5 then divide by 20.

B. Add 5 and 8 then subtract from 20.

C. Add 20 and 5 then subtract the total from 8.

D. Add 8 and 5 then subtract 5 from the sum.

2. Jennifer is making brownies for 4 other teachers on her block. She plans to put 5 large chocolate chips on each brownie. If she wants each teacher to have 6 brownies, how many chocolate chips will Jennifer need? (*Show your work. Write your final answer on the line.*)

_____

1. Mr. Simpson bought a used car for his daughter. The car cost $9,499. The tax on the car came to $488. He made a down payment of $2,575. How much money does Mr. Simpson still owe? (*Show your work. Circle the letter of the correct choice.*)

    A. $9,987

    B. $12,562

    C. $2,087

    D. $7,412

2. Leslie has 35 crayons. He and 4 students in his class are sharing them. How can Leslie find how many crayons each person will get? (*Circle the letter of the correct choice.*)

    A. Add 35 and 4   **C.** Divide 35 by 5

    B. Subtract 4 from 35   **D.** Multiply 35 by 5

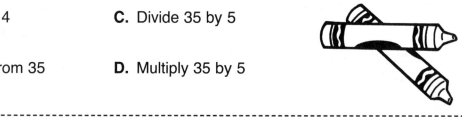

1. Jim bought 3 video games for $21. Two of the video games cost the same amount while the third cost $5. How much did each of the other video games cost? (*Show your work. Circle the letter for the correct choice.*)

    A. $9

    B. $8

    C. $7

    D. $6

2. Billy owned 26,492 acres of farm land. During 1992, he purchased another 5,424 acres from his cousin. In 2002, he sold 10,053 acres to a developer. How many acres does Billy now own? (Show your work. *Write your final answer on the line.*)

                                                                   _____

Name _____ **Date** _____

Warm-Up 51

1. Coach Kearny bought shirts for his basketball players. He bought 19 small shirts that cost $6 each, 25 medium shirts that cost $8 each, and 34 large shirts that cost $12 each. How much money did Coach Kearney spend altogether? (*Show your work. Write your final answer on the line.*)

_____

2. Cody earns $5 an hour. Last week he worked 36 hours. This week, Cody worked 14 more hours than he did last week. How much money did Cody earn during both weeks? (*Show your work. Write your final answer on the line.*)

_____

Name _____ **Date** _____

Warm-Up 52

1. Duane mows lawns during the summer. For each yard he mows, he earns $25. Over the summer, Duane mowed 65 lawns. How much money did Duane earn altogether? (*Show your work. Write your final answer on the line.*)

_____

2. Maci and Ty are saving for a new trampoline. They are combining their money by putting what they save into a piggy bank. They counted their money and found that they have saved $75. Ty put $25 more in the piggy bank than Maci. How much money did each person contribute to the piggy bank? (*Write your answers in the boxes.*)

MACI	TY

DAILY
Warm-Up 53

Name _____ Date _____

1. Ms. Mason is a fourth grade teacher. For the class party, Ms. Mason wants to buy 2 pencils for each of the 21 students in her class. She can buy packages for $5.99. There are 12 pencils in each package. Four of the pencils are yellow, 4 of the are red, and 4 of the pencils are blue. How many packages of pencils must Ms. Mason buy for each student in her class to get exactly 2? (*Show your work. Circle the letter of the correct answer.*)

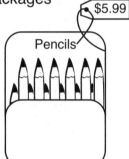

A. 2   **C.** 4

B. 3   **D.** 5

2. Jackie is watching people waiting for the elevator. She counted the number of people waiting and found there were 120 people waiting to ride the elevator to the 12th floor. There are 4 elevators that hold a maximum of 15 people each. If no more people get in line, how many people will be waiting after the next ride fills up? (*Show your work. Write your final answer on the line.*)

_____

DAILY
Warm-Up 54

Name _____ Date _____

1. Lee bought donuts for his employees at work. A quarter of the donuts were chocolate. If Lee bought 28 donuts, how many chocolate donuts did he buy? (*Show your work. Circle the letter of the correct answer.*)

A. 112

B. 7

C. 21

D. 35

2. Sandra wrote the problems below on the board. Which problem will give the smallest answer? (*Circle the letter of the correct answer.*)

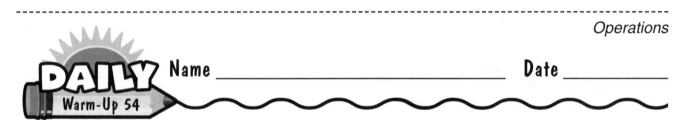

A. $6\overline{)96}$ B. $6 + 96$ C. 6×96 D. $96 - 6$

Name _____ Date _____

Warm-Up 55

1. Mrs. Chilek has 22 students in her class. Today, 2 of the 22 students are absent. Mrs. Chilek plans to create 5 reading groups from the students present. If there are an equal number of students in each group, how many students are in each group? (*Show your work. Write your final answer on the line.*)

_____

2. Kyle bought 4 packages of notebook paper. There are 50 sheets in the 1st package, 100 sheets in the 2nd package, 150 sheets in the 3rd package, and 200 sheets in the 4th package. Kyle already had 75 sheets of paper in his notebook. How many total sheets of notebook paper does Kyle now have? (*Show your work. Write your final answer on the line.*)

_____

Name _____ Date _____

Warm-Up 56

1. Look at the table. June scored a total of 335 points on 4 math tests. She scored 89 points on the first test, 90 points on the second test, and 91 points on the third test. How many points did she score on the fourth test? (*Fill in your final answer on the table.*)

Test	Points
First	89
Second	90
Third	91
Fourth	
Total	335

Show your work.

2. Which model below shows the product of 6 x 3?
(*Circle the letter of the correct model.*)

A.

B.

C.

D.

DAILY
Warm-Up 57

Name _____   Date _____

1. Vera sells watermelons she raises on her grandparents' farm. Yesterday, Vera sold 4 extra large watermelons for $12 each, 5 large watermelons for $8 each, and 19 small watermelons for $4 each. Today, Vera sold twice as many extra large, large, and small watermelons as she did yesterday. However, Vera sold 9 medium watermelons for $6 each. How much money did Vera earn on both days? (*Show your work. Write your final answer on the line.*)

_____

2. Jane had 692 colored beads. Her cousin gave her 329 more. She wants to make a necklace that will have 1,420 beads. How many more beads must Jane collect to be able to make her necklace? (*Show your work. Write your final answer on the line.*)

_____

DAILY
Warm-Up 58

Name _____   Date _____

1. Carol is selling boxes of candy bars for a fundraiser. She sold 12 boxes. There are 24 candy bars in each box. Which equation could Carol use to find out how many total candy bars she sold? (*Circle the letter of the correct answer.*)

A. 24 − 12

C. 24 x 12

B. 24 + 12

D. 24 ÷ 12

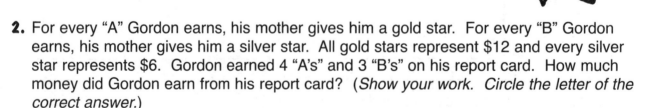

2. For every "A" Gordon earns, his mother gives him a gold star. For every "B" Gordon earns, his mother gives him a silver star. All gold stars represent $12 and every silver star represents $6. Gordon earned 4 "A's" and 3 "B's" on his report card. How much money did Gordon earn from his report card? (*Show your work. Circle the letter of the correct answer.*)

A. $60

B. $66

C. $45

D. $18

1. Paul decided to save the money he earned. The first week, he saved $9. The second week, he doubled what he saved the first week. The third week, he saved 3 times as much as he did for the first week. How much total money did Paul save during all three weeks? (*Show your work. Circle the letter of the correct answer.*)

   A. $9

   B. $54

   C. $67

   D. Not Given

2. Coach Kearney had batting practice today. Each player got to swing at the ball 7 times. If 9 players came to practice, how many balls were pitched? (*Show your work. Write your final answer on the line.*)

_____

----

1. Mrs. Hargrove buys apples by the basket. Small baskets hold 18 apples. A middle-size basket holds 32 apples. The largest basket holds 48 apples. If Mrs. Hargrove bought one small basket, one middle-size basket, and one large basket, how many total apples did Mrs. Hargrove buy? (*Show your work. Write your final answer on the line.*)

_____

2. Mrs. Hinojosa made 189 jars of strawberry jelly. She sold 19 to a neighbor and 38 to each of her 3 friends. How many jars of strawberry jelly does Mrs. Hinojosa now have? (*Show your work. Circle the letter of the correct answer.*)

   A. 56

   B. 170

   C. 133

   D. 129

Name _____ Date _____

1. Jackie received $50 for her birthday. Wanting to buy school clothes, she emptied her piggy bank and went shopping. She bought breakfast that cost $6. She bought 3 shirts that cost $12 each and 6 pairs of jeans for $30 each. When she arrived back at home, she had only $25 left. With how much money did Jackie start her shopping? (*Show your work. Write your final answer on the line.*)

2. Jane bought 3 hats for $8 each and 4 new shirts that cost $12 each. Which number sentence can be used to find the total amount of money in dollars that Jane spent? (*Circle the letter of the correct answer.*)

   A. 8 x 4 =

   B. 24 + 48 =

   C. 12 + 8 =

   D. 16 + 12 =

Name _____ Date _____

1. Robert bought 12 cases of chips. There were 35 bags of chips in each case. How many total bags of chips did Robert buy? (*Show your work. Write your final answer on the line.*)

_____

2. Marsha baby-sits for her neighbors' kids on two separate nights. She earned $12 for the first night and $18 for the second. She also cleaned her parents' house and earned $15 more. Which expression shows how to find the total amount of money in dollars that Marsha earned? (*Circle the letter of the correct answer.*)

   A. 2 x 12 + 18   **B.** 2 + 12 + 33   **C.** 12 + 18   **D.** 12 + 18 + 15

Operations

Answer Key

Warm-Up 1
1. 7 packages
2. C

Warm-Up 2
1. B
2. $376

Warm-Up 3
1. 4 hours
2. 8 rows

Warm-Up 4
1. 48 grapes
2. D

Warm-Up 5
1. 450 sheets
2. 5 gallons

Warm-Up 6
1. 6 pages
2. 2 pencils

Warm-Up 7
1. 132 hair ribbons
2. D

Warm-Up 8
1. B
2. 5 miles

Warm-Up 9
1. C
2. B

Warm-Up 10
1. 60 stuffed bears
2. 37 birds

Warm-Up 11
1. D
2. B

Warm-Up 12
1. 392 tomato plants
2. C

Warm-Up 13
1. C
2. C

Warm-Up 14
1. 9 cars
2. $17

Warm-Up 15
1. 887 bags
2. 64¢

Warm-Up 16
1. $1,700
2. 176 more miles

Warm-Up 17
1. $570
2. A

Warm-Up 18
1. 22 buckets
2. 212 cars

Warm-Up 19
1. D
2. $10 + $10 + $10 + $10 + $5 + $5 + $5
   Total Amount Received: $55

Warm-Up 20
1. 21 students
2. C

Warm-Up 21
1. B
2. 36 candy bars

Warm-Up 22
1. $1,575
2. 192 cans

Warm-Up 23
1. $147
2. 360 orange and grape sodas

Warm-Up 24
1. B
2. C

Warm-Up 25
1. A
2. B

Warm-Up 26
1. 7
2. D

Warm-Up 27
1. 324 photos
2. C

Warm-Up 28
1.
$$8\overline{)95} = 11 \text{ R7}$$
$$-8$$
$$15$$
$$-8$$
$$7$$
2. 15 sweaters

Warm-Up 29
1. C
2. 1,356 miles

Warm-Up 30
1. $146.29
2. C

Warm-Up 31
1. D
2. 26 minutes

Warm-Up 32
1. 2 groups of 9, 3 left over
2. $202

Warm-Up 33
1. 24
2. 131 baseball cards

Warm-Up 34
1. 84
2. C

Warm-Up 35
1. 1,519 flowers
2. C

Warm-Up 36
1. B
2. 216 cans

Warm-Up 37
1. 85 tomatoes
2. B

Warm-Up 38
1. Multiply 6 x 2 to find how many Presley has.
2. C

Warm-Up 39
1. 31 apples
2. B

Answer Key

Warm-Up 40
1. D
2. B

Warm-Up 41
1. 12 letters
2. 42 buttons

Warm-Up 42
1. 7 markers
2. $30

Warm-Up 43
1. $95
2. 1 = C
   2 = D
   3 = B
   4 = A

Warm-Up 44
1. $25
2. C

Warm-Up 45
1. $13.61
2. $5.25

Warm-Up 46
1. $245
2. $4,750

Warm-Up 47
1. 1,855 paper clips
2. C

Warm-Up 48
1. B
2. 120 chocolate chips

Warm-Up 49
1. D
2. C

Warm-Up 50
1. B
2. 21,863 acres

Warm-Up 51
1. $722
2. $430

Warm-Up 52
1. $1,625
2. Ty = $50
   Maci = $25

Warm-Up 53
1. C
2. 60 people

Warm-Up 54
1. B
2. A

Warm-Up 55
1. 4 students
2. 575 sheets

Warm-Up 56
1. 89 + 90 + 91 = 270,
   335 − 270 = 65
   65
2. C

Warm-Up 57
1. $546
2. 399 beads

Warm-Up 58
1. C
2. B

Warm-Up 59
1. B
2. 63 balls

Warm-Up 60
1. 98 apples
2. A

Warm-Up 61
1. $247
2. B

Warm-Up 62
1. 420 bags
2. D

MEASUREMENT AND GEOMETRY

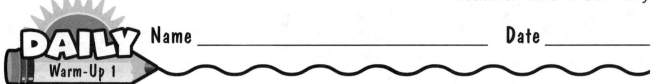

Name _____ **Date** _____

1. Circle the letter in the name below that has **NO** perpendicular lines.

HEATH

2. Frank needs 6 yards of garden trim for his vegetable garden. He can buy the trim in 4 ft., 6 ft., 9 ft., and 12 ft. pieces. Which answer choice below would be the best purchase for Frank to make? (*Circle the correct letter.*)

A. 3 four-foot pieces

B. 3 six-foot pieces

C. 3 nine-foot pieces

D. 3 twelve-foot pieces

Name _____ **Date** _____

1. Mrs. Watkins bought 1 gallon of milk yesterday. How many pints of milk are in 1 gallon? (*Write your answer on the line.*)

_____

2. Which answer choice below is a correct definition of **congruency**? (*Circle the correct letter.*)

A. same shape, different size   **C.** same shape, same size

B. same size, different shape   **D.** not given

DAILY
Warm-Up 3

Name _____ Date _____

1. Maci's cat has 3 kittens. Her favorite kitten weighed one-half pound when born. How many ounces did the kitten weigh? (*Write your answer on the line.*)

_____

2. To what type of lines are the arrows pointing? (*Write your answer on the line.*)

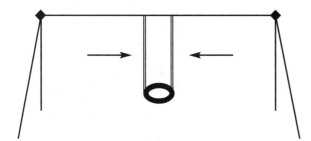

_____

DAILY
Warm-Up 4

Name _____ Date _____

1. Larry is restoring an old car. He needs to purchase 5 yards of fabric for the seats. The fabric is priced by the foot only. How many feet of fabric does Larry need? (*Show your work. Write your final answer on the line.*)

_____

2. Which of these figures has **NO** vertices? (*Circle the letter of the correct answer.*)

A. 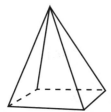 **B.** 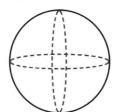 **C.** 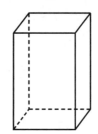 **D.**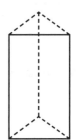

DAILY Warm-Up 5

Name _____ Date _____

1. Sue is decorating the top edges of a small box with trim, but she is uncertain about the length needed. If she places the trim on all four sides (the perimeter) of the box shown below, what would be the length in inches she will need to complete this task? (*Write your answer on the line.*)

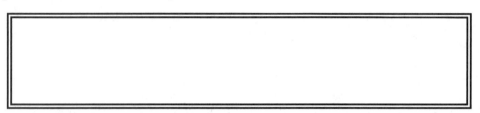

_____

2. Which figures appear to be **congruent**?
(*Circle the letter of the correct response.*)

A. 1 and 3   **C.** 1 and 2

B. 2 and 3   **D.** 3 and 5

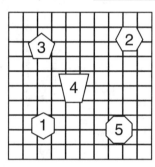

DAILY Warm-Up 6

Name _____ Date _____

1. Kevin is playing baseball with his friends. There are 90 feet from base to base. If Kevin hits the ball and makes it to 3rd base, how many feet did Kevin run? (*Show your work. Write your final answer on the line.*)

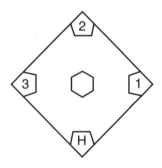

_____

2. Fred bought a rope that was 6 yards long. He needs 15 feet of rope to make a swing for his daughter. What should Fred do first to find out if he has enough rope to equal 15 feet? (*Circle the letter of the correct response.*)

A. Multiply 15 by 6   **C.** Multiply 6 by 3   **B.** Multiply 15 by 3   **D.** Multiply 15 by 12

DAILY Warm-Up 7

Name _____ Date _____

1. What type of angle best describes angle *G*? (*Write your answer on the line.*)

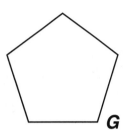

G

_____

2. What angle is shown below? (*Circle the letter of the correct answer.*)

A. right angle   **C.** acute angle

B. obtuse angle   **D.** bent angle

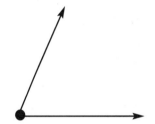

DAILY Warm-Up 8

Name _____ Date _____

1. How many circular bases does the cylinder have? (*Write your final answer on the line.*)

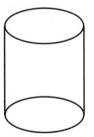

_____

2. The figure here is an example of a . . . (*Circle the letter of the correct term.*)

A. rotation

B. reflection

C. translation

D. not given

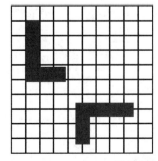

DAILY
Warm-Up 9

Name _____   Date _____

1. Which of the following models is **NOT** a reflection? (*Circle the letter of the correct answer.*)

A. Pq   B. qP   C. PP   D. P b

2. Cody needs exactly 30 yards of rope to make a swing for his niece and nephew. When he went to the hardware store, he could purchase the rope in 5 ft., 8 ft., 10 ft., or 12 ft. pieces. Which answer below would be the most reasonable choice for Cody to make? (*Circle the correct letter.*)

A. two 5-ft. pieces   **C.** nine 10-ft. pieces

B. three 8-ft. pieces   **D.** three 12-ft. pieces

- -

DAILY
Warm-Up 10

Name _____   Date _____

1. Bethany bought 15 yards of yellow lace to use on a quilt she was making with her grandmother. She used 40 feet of lace on the quilt. How many feet of yellow lace does Bethany have left? (*Show your work. Write your final answer on the line.*)

_____

2. Jim works after school every other school day. If he worked on March 6, on which of the following days will he **NOT** work? (*Circle the letter of the correct answer.*)

A. March 12   **C.** March 21

B. March 16   **D.** March 28

March						
SUNDAY	MONDAY	TUESDAY	WEDNESDAY	THURSDAY	FRIDAY	SATURDAY
				1	2	3
4	5	6	7	8	9	10
11	12	13	14	15	16	17
18	19	20	21	22	23	24
25	26	27	28	29	30	

DAILY **Warm-Up 11** Name _____ Date _____

1. Lee is making 5 bird feeders of different heights for his mother's yard. His mother wants 400 grams of feed for each bird feeder. How many kilograms of birdseed does Lee use altogether? (*Show your work. Write your final answer on the line.*)

_____

2. Wanda has 24 pints of jam she wants to store in boxes. Eight pints will fit in 1 box. How many total boxes will Wanda need to store all 24 pints of jam? (*Show your work. Circle the letter of the correct answer.*)

A. 3   **C.** 27

B. 21   **D.** 72

DAILY **Warm-Up 12** Name _____ Date _____

1. Which figure below is **NOT** an example of a translation? (*Circle the letter of the correct choice.*)

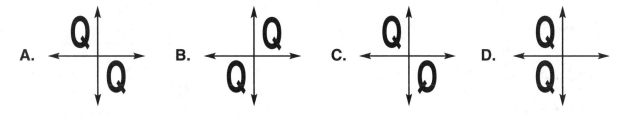

2. Which answer choice below does **NOT** belong with the others? (*Circle the letter of the correct choice.*)

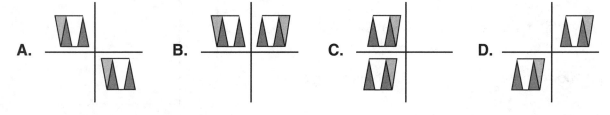

Warm-Up 13

1. Terry filled her 8-ounce coffee cup to the top and poured it in one of the cylinders below. Into which cylinder did Terry pour her coffee? (*Circle the letter of the correct choice.*)

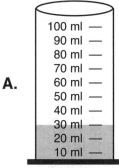

A.
100 ml —
90 ml —
80 ml —
70 ml —
60 ml —
50 ml —
40 ml —
30 ml —
20 ml —
10 ml —

B.
100 ml —
90 ml —
80 ml —
70 ml —
60 ml —
50 ml —
40 ml —
30 ml —
20 ml —
10 ml —

C.
100 ml —
90 ml —
80 ml —
70 ml —
60 ml —
50 ml —
40 ml —
30 ml —
20 ml —
10 ml —

D.
100 ml —
90 ml —
80 ml —
70 ml —
60 ml —
50 ml —
40 ml —
30 ml —
20 ml —
10 ml —

2. Sharee bought 1 gallon of milk. She used 1 pint to make a dessert for her family. How many pints of milk does Sharee still have? (*Show your work. Write your final answer on the line.*)

_____

Warm-Up 14

1. What transformation is shown on the model below? (*Circle the letter of the correct choice.*)

   A. rotation   **C.** reflection

   B. translation   **D.** not given

2. The drawing below is an example of what kind of angle? (*Circle the letter of the correct description.*)

   A. straight angle   **C.** acute angle

   B. right angle   **D.** obtuse angle

Name _____ **Date** _____

Warm-Up 15

1. For the past week, Kane measured temperatures "High" and "Low" for a science project. The chart shows his findings. Based on the chart, what is the difference between the high temperature on Monday and the low temperature on Friday? (*Circle the letter of the correct choice.*)

Day	High	Low
Sunday	97°	58°
Monday	102°	64°
Tuesday	98°	63°
Wednesday	93°	54°
Thursday	95°	60°
Friday	97°	65°
Saturday	88°	59°

A. 37°   **C.** 38°

B. 65°   **D.** 32°

2. Cody played four games of a math board game. Each game lasted the same amount time. If all four games lasted a total of 2 hours and 24 minutes, how many minutes did each game last? (*Show your work. Circle the letter of the correct answer.*)

A. 120 minutes

B. 36 minutes

C. 44 minutes

D. 144 minutes

Name _____ **Date** _____

Warm-Up 16

1. Which two shapes are congruent? (*Circle the letter of the correct answer.*)

A. Shape 1 and 2

B. Shape 2 and 3

C. Shape 1 and 3

D. Shape 1 and 4

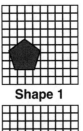

Shape 1   **Shape 3**

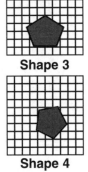

Shape 2   **Shape 4**

2. Which diagram shows a translation? (*Circle the letter of the correct diagram.*)

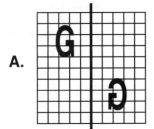
A.

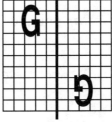
B.

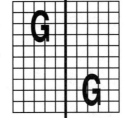
C.

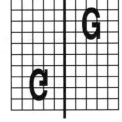
D.

Name _____ **Date** _____

Warm-Up 17

1. Sue wanted to put pink lace around two matching square picture mirrors. She knew she needed 15 inches for each side of the mirror. How many total inches of lace would Sue need to purchase to put lace around the perimeter of both mirrors? (*Write your answer on the line.*)

Frame 1   **Frame 2**

_____

2. Which is **NOT** a correct unit for measuring length? (*Circle the letter of the correct answer.*)

A. millimeter   **B.** centimeter   **C.** milliliter   **D.** yards

---

Name _____ **Date** _____

Warm-Up 18

1. Look at the house. Use your ruler to find the length of the house in feet. (*Then circle the letter of the correct length below.*)

A. 75 feet

B. 150 feet

C. 225 feet

D. not given

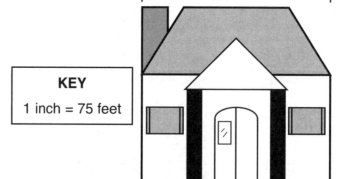

KEY

1 inch = 75 feet

2. Which answer below is **NOT** a correct unit for measuring weight? (*Circle the letter of the correct answer.*)

A. pounds   **B.** grams   **C.** centimeters   **D.** kilograms

Name _____   Date _____

1. Jake and Jeffrey love to fish. Yesterday, Jeffrey caught a fish that weighed 24 ounces. How many pounds and ounces does that fish weigh? (*Show your work. Write your answer on the line.*)

_____

2. Jim wants to measure the weight of his computer. Which unit of measurement should Jim use? (*Circle the letter of the correct unit.*)

A. tons   **B.** pounds   **C.** ounces   **D.** feet

Name _____   Date _____

1. If you wanted to measure the length of a fly, which unit of measurement would you use? (*Circle the letter of correct response below.*)

A. yards   **B.** ounces   **C.** millimeters   **D.** pounds

2. Use a ruler to find the length (in feet) of the line segments from start to finish.

| 1 cm = 4 ft. |

Start

Finish

Total Length: _____ feet

DAILY Warm-Up 21

Name _____ Date _____

1. Jim's truck delivers laundry during the week. What is the most appropriate unit to find the weight of Jim's truck? (*Circle the letter of the correct answer.*)

   A. yards   **C.** tons

   B. pounds   **D.** feet

2. Which is the best estimate of the capacity of a mop bucket? (*Circle the letter of the correct answer.*)

   A. 15 grams   **B.** 15 liters   **C.** 15 ounces   **D.** 15 pounds

---

DAILY Warm-Up 22

Name _____ Date _____

1. Which shape below is **NOT** a solid figure? (*Circle the letter of the correct answer.*)

A.    **B.**    **C.**    **D.**

2. George is measuring an object's length in millimeters. Which object is he most likely measuring? (*Circle the letter of the best response.*)

   A. the length of a paintbrush   **C.** the length of a pool

   B. the length of a thumb tack   **D.** the length of a dog

Name _____ **Date** _____

1. Circle the letter in the name below that has the **most** lines of symmetry.

YOLANDA

2. What is the best estimate of the weight of a fifth grade student? (*Circle the letter of the correct answer.*)

A. 70 ounces   **B.** 70 pounds   **C.** 70 kilometers   **D.** 7,000 pounds

----

Name _____ **Date** _____

1. Look at the clocks. Maci baby-sits her brother from 8:30 A.M. to 11:15 A.M. each day during the summer. How long does she baby-sit each day? (*Write your answer on the line.*)

Start

Finish

_____

2. Which two sides are **parallel** on the rectangle?
(*Circle the letter of the correct answer.*)

A. Sides *M* and *N*

B. Sides *N* and *O*

C. Sides *P* and *N*

D. Sides *P* and *M*

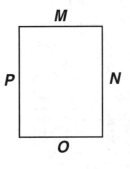

Name _____ **Date** _____

1. Which transformation is represented by the model?
(*Circle the letter of the correct answer.*)

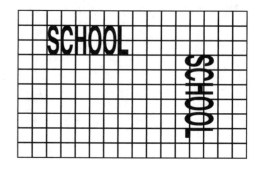

   A. Slide

   B. Rotation

   C. Flip

   D. Not Given

2. Which shape below does **NOT** belong with the others? (*Circle the letter of the correct shape.*)

 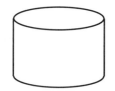 **B.** 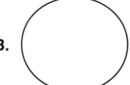 **C.** 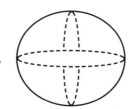 **D.**

Name _____ **Date** _____

1. Which statement is **true** about a cube? (*Circle the correct letter choice.*)

   A. It has 6 vertices, 8 edges, and 12 faces.

   B. It has 12 vertices, 6 faces, and 8 edges.

   C. It has 6 faces, 8 vertices, and 12 edges.

   D. It has 12 faces, 8 edges, and 6 vertices.

2. Which answer choice below shows a reflection of the letter **P**? (*Circle the correct letter choice.*)

A. 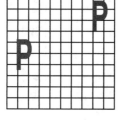 **B.** 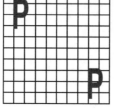 **C.** 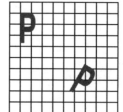 **D.**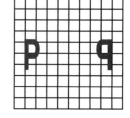

Name _____ **Date** _____

1. I have 12 edges, 6 faces, and 8 vertices. What am I? (*Write your answer on the line.*)

_____

2. What is the **area** of the rectangle below? (*Write your answer on the line.*)

9 ft.

5 ft.

_____

Name _____ **Date** _____

1. The perimeter of rectangle **X** is how many centimeters greater than the perimeter of rectangle **Y**? (*Write your answer on the line.*)

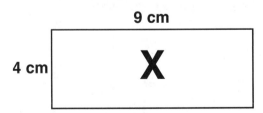

_____

2. Jim is starting a new business cleaning pools. He is taking out an ad with the local newspaper. What is the perimeter in centimeters of the ad Jim took out advertising his new business? (*Write your answer on the line.*)

Jim's Pool Cleaning
Check Chlorine
Vacuum
Water Treatment
Reasonable Prices
Call 543-POOL

_____

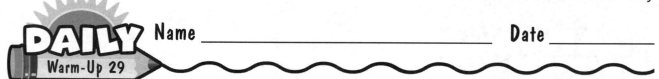

Name _____ **Date** _____

1. Which is **true** about a triangular prism? (*Circle the letter of the true answer.*)

    A. It has 6 faces, 9 edges, and 6 vertices.

    B. It has 9 edges, 6 vertices, and 5 faces.

    C. It has 9 faces, 5 edges, and 6 vertices.

    D. It has 6 faces, 5 edges, and 9 vertices.

2. What angle is represented by the letter *G*? (*Circle the letter of the correct answer.*)

    A. The letter *G* is a right angle.

    B. The letter *G* is an obtuse angle.

    C. The letter *G* is an acute angle.

    D. The letter *G* is a point angle.

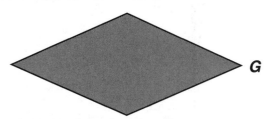

G

Name _____ **Date** _____

1. Lee's mother wants to grow tomatoes. Lee agrees to make her a small vegetable garden. The garden measures 4 feet long and 5 feet wide. What is the area of the vegetable garden? (*Show your work. Circle the letter of the correct answer.*)

    A. 8 square feet

    B. 9 square feet

    C. 18 square feet

    D. 20 square feet

2. Lucy works from 2:45 P.M. to 5:15 P.M. each day. How long does Lucy work each day? (*Write your answer on the line.*)

_____

Name _____ **Date** _____

1. Which is the most reasonable estimate for the amount of the container? (*Circle the letter for the best response.*)

    A. 1 gallon

    B. 1 pint

    C. 1 quart

    D. 1 milliliter

2. Draw a regular **pentagon** in the space below.

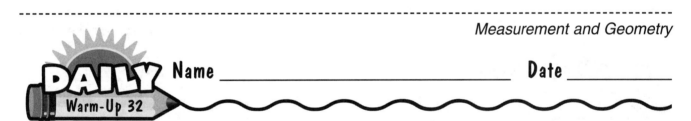

Name _____ **Date** _____

1. Frank needs 20 feet of rope to make a swing for his son. He can buy the rope in 6-yard, 8-yard, 10-yard, or 15-yard lengths. Which would be the smartest purchase for Frank to make? (*Circle the letter of the best response.*)

    A. Buy two 15-yard lengths.

    B. Buy one 8-yard length.

    C. Buy two 10-yard lengths.

    D. Buy two 6-yard lengths.

2. Mark drew this shape on the board. He challenged his friend to correctly label the parts of the shape. If Mark's friend did this correctly, what labels did he write? (*Write your answer on the lines.*)

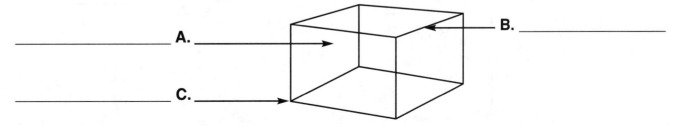

_____ **A.**   **B.** _____

_____ **C.**

DAILY
Warm-Up 33

Name _____ Date _____

1. Which letter has a line of symmetry? (*Circle the letter choice for the correct response.*)

A. **G**   B. **T**   C. **R**   D. **F**

2. Label the angles to which the arrows are pointing on the pencil.

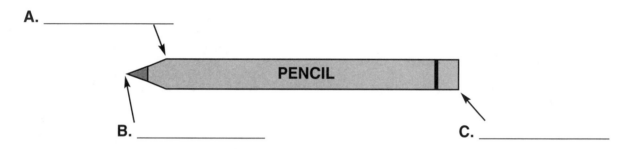

A. _____

B. _____   C. _____

DAILY
Warm-Up 34

Name _____ Date _____

1. The **capacity** of the spoon could best be measured in which of the following units? (*Circle the letter of the correct response.*)

A. pounds   C. milliliters

B. liters   D. quarts

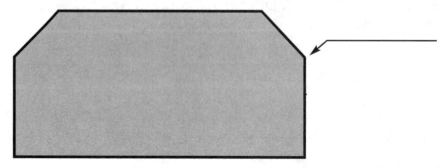

2. To what type of angle is the arrow pointing on the drawing below? (*Write your answer on the line.*)

Warm-Up 35

1. Look at the pattern below. If you were to cut out the solid lines and fold the dashed lines, what three-dimensional figure would you make? (*Write your answer on the line.*)

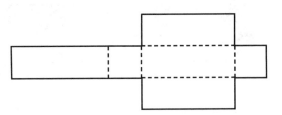

_____

2. Answer **TRUE** or **FALSE** to the following statements.

A._____   The width of a door is about 1 meter.

B._____   The weight of a sheet of paper should be measured in pounds.

C._____   A good way to measure the height of a tree is in meters.

D._____   Your math book weighs about 1 gram.

Warm-Up 36

1. On what coordinates is the cube? (*Write your answer on the line.*)

_____

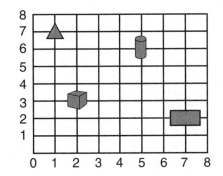

2. How many lines of symmetry does the rectangle have? (*Write your answer on the line.*)

_____

Name _____ **Date** _____

DAILY Warm-Up 37

1. How long is the marker in centimeters? (*Write your answer on the line.*)

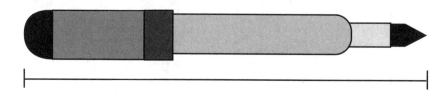

_____

2. Which of the following has the same number of vertices? (*Circle the letter of the correct answer.*)

A. cube and rectangular prism

C. cylinder and rectangular prism

B. cube and cylinder

D. sphere and rectangular prism

Name _____ **Date** _____

DAILY Warm-Up 38

1. How long is the screw in centimeters? (*Write your answer on the line.*)

_____

2. Which shape has the most perpendicular lines? (*Circle the letter of the correct shape.*)

A. 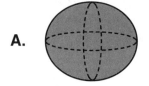   **B.**    **C.**   **D.**

Name _____ **Date** _____

1. What tool should Mary use to measure the weight of a watermelon? (*Circle the letter of the correct response.*)

   A. thermometer   **B.** ruler   **C.** scale   **D.** not given

2. Jack's grandfather raises horses. Jack's grandfather told him that a horse's height is measured in a unit called a hand. A hand measures 4 inches. He asked Jack, "What is the height in inches of a horse that measures 12 hands?" If Jack answered correctly, what answer below did Jack give? (*Show your work. Circle the letter of the correct answer.*)

   A. 45 inches   **C.** 50 inches

   B. 48 inches   **D.** 52 inches

Name _____ **Date** _____

1. Jane cut a strip of paper that was 30 centimeters long. How many millimeters long was the strip of paper Jane cut? (*Show your work. Write your answer on the line.*)

   _____

2. Which statement about the figure is true? (*Circle the letter of the correct response.*)

   A. Side *WY* is parallel to side *WZ*.

   B. Side *WY* is parallel to side *XZ*.

   C. Side *WX* is perpendicular to side *YZ*.

   D. Side *WX* is parallel to side *XZ*.

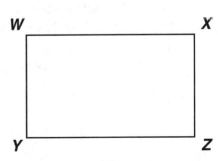

Name _____ **Date** _____

Warm-Up 41

1. Which letter on the number line does point $6\frac{1}{4}$ best represent? (*Circle the letter of the correct response.*)

A. *W*

B. *X*

C. *Y*

D. *Z*

2. Mary's birthday is in three months. If this is the month of February, in what month will Mary's birthday be? (*Write your answer on the line.*)

_____

Name _____ **Date** _____

Warm-Up 42

1. Which of the following statements is true about congruent figures? (*Circle the letter of the correct response.*)

A. The objects have the same size and same shape.

B. The objects are the same size and different shape.

C. The objects are different shape and same size.

D. Not Given

2. Mike's mother took him and his sister to the store to buy a new toy. Mike's new toy weighed 1 pound 3 ounces. His sister's toy weighed 2 pounds 4 ounces. How many more ounces does Mike's sister's toy weigh?

Explain: _____

_____

_____

DAILY
Warm-Up 43

Name _____

Date _____

1. Howard made 3 flowerbeds in his backyard. They do not touch each other. Each flowerbed was in the shape of an octagon. How many total sides were on all 3 flowerbeds? (*Write your answer on the line.*)

_____

2. Wanda is making dough for kolaches she is making for a party. Wanda needs 2 tablespoons of salt for every 5 pounds of dough. Wanda is making 15 pounds of kolache dough. How many tablespoons of salt does she need? (*Circle the letter of the correct answer.*)

A. 2 tablespoons

B. 4 tablespoons

C. 6 tablespoons

D. 8 tablespoons

DAILY
Warm-Up 44

Name _____

Date _____

1. When Jason left for work, the temperature was 32°F. By lunchtime, the temperature had risen 18 degrees. What was the temperature at lunchtime? (*Write your answer on the line .*)

_____

2. Jim is putting holiday lights around the greenhouse in his yard. The greenhouse is in the shape of a rectangle that measures 6 feet wide and 8 feet long. How many feet of holiday lights will Jim need to complete this task? (*Write your answer on the line.*)

8 ft.

6 ft.

_____

Warm-Up 45

1. Margo is making hamburgers for a cookout. She will use 4 ounces of meat in each hamburger. How many pounds of meat will she need to make 20 hamburgers? (*Show your work. Write your final answer on the line.*)

_____

2. Which of the following would most likely measure about 4 meters? (*Circle the letter of the best answer.*)

A. the length of a car

C. the length of a pencil

B. the height of an ice tea glass

D. the length of a computer keyboard

Warm-Up 46

1. Katie has volleyball practice every other day (including weekends). If practice began on June 2, which of the following days will she **NOT** have practice? (*Circle the letter of the correct answer.*)

A. June 10

B. June 30

C. June 15

D. June 14

June						
SUNDAY	MONDAY	TUESDAY	WEDNESDAY	THURSDAY	FRIDAY	SATURDAY
				1	2	3
4	5	6	7	8	9	10
11	12	13	14	15	16	17
18	19	20	21	22	23	24
25	26	27	28	29	30	

2. How many millimeters are in 2 centimeters? (*Write your answer on the line.*)

_____

Name _____ **Date** _____

Warm-Up 47

1. Sue went to the store and bought a 2-pound box of laundry detergent. She used 4 ounces for each of the 2 loads of clothes she washed. How many ounces of laundry detergent does Sue have left? (*Show your work. Write your final answer on the line.*)

_____

2. Sam drank 500 milliliters of juice from a 1-liter carton he bought at the store. How much juice does Sam have left in the carton? (*Show your work. Write your final answer on the line.*)

_____

- -

Name _____ **Date** _____

Warm-Up 48

1. Agnes has 36 pints of jam she wants to store in boxes. Four pints will fit in 1 box. How many total boxes will Agnes need to store all 36 pints of jam? (*Show your work. Circle the letter of the correct answer.*)

A. 9

B. 32

C. 40

D. 84

2. Roy bought 40 feet of streamers to be used at the senior prom. Seven yards were used in decorating the inside and 3 more yards were used outside. How many feet of streamers does Roy have left? (*Show your work. Write your answer on the line.*)

_____

DAILY Warm-Up 49

Name _____ Date _____

1. Samantha bought a new book that weighed 1 pound 8 ounces. How many ounces did the book weigh? (*Show your work. Write your answer on the line.*)

_____

2. Cody ran the 100-yard dash in 48 seconds. Jimmy ran the 100-yard dash 12 seconds slower than Cody. What was Jimmy's time? (*Write your answer on the line.*)

_____

DAILY Warm-Up 50

Name _____ Date _____

1. Pete drew a parallelogram on the chalkboard. How many sets of parallel lines does a parallelogram have? (*Circle the letter of the correct response.*)

A. 1   **B.** 2   **C.** 3   **D.** Not Given

2. Rosa is making a garden that measures 15 meters wide and 20 meters long. What is the area of Rosa's garden? (*Show your work. Write your answer on the line.*)

_____

DAILY
Warm-Up 51

Name _____   Date _____

1. Jack goes to the gym every other day. If he went to the gym on February 4, on which of the following days will he **NOT** have to go to the gym? (*Circle the letter of the correct response.*)

   A. February 12   **C.** February 21

   B. February 18   **D.** February 24

February

SUNDAY	MONDAY	TUESDAY	WEDNESDAY	THURSDAY	FRIDAY	SATURDAY
1	2	3	4	5	6	7
8	9	10	11	12	13	14
15	16	17	18	19	20	21
22	23	24	25	26	27	28
29						

2. What is the area of the polygon drawn on the grid in square inches? (*Write your answer on the line.*)

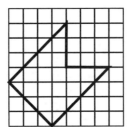

   _____

DAILY
Warm-Up 52

Name _____   Date _____

1. How wide is the butterfly from wing to wing, in inches? (*Write your answer on the line.*)

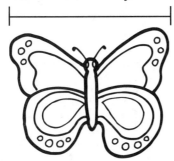

   _____

2. Jack bought a watermelon that weighed 4 pounds. How many ounces did the watermelon weigh? (*Show your work. Circle the letter of the correct amount.*)

   A. 16 ounces   **C.** 48 ounces

   B. 32 ounces   **D.** 64 ounces

1. Jack is trying to find the length of his new baseball bat. Which measurement below is about the same as the length of a baseball bat? (*Circle the letter of the correct response.*)

A. 1 kilometer   **B.** 1 meter   **C.** 1 millimeter   **D.** 1 inch

2. Jim is making a garden that measures 12 meters wide by 20 meters long. What is the area of the garden Jim is making? (*Show your work. Circle the letter of the correct response.*)

A. 32 square meters

B. 120 square meters

C. 8 square meters

D. 240 square meters

1. The sides of the pentagon shown here are all the same. What is the perimeter of the pentagon? (*Write your answer on the line.*)

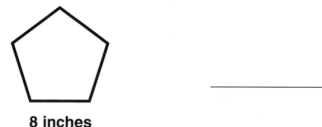

_____

8 inches

2. Janice is washing dishes after Thanksgiving dinner with her family. What is the best estimate of the capacity of a kitchen sink? (*Circle the letter of the best response.*)

A. 6 feet   **C.** 6 pints

B. 6 gallons   **D.** 6 milliliters

Name _____ **Date** _____

Warm-Up 55

1. Jack drew an octagon, hexagon, pentagon, and parallelogram on the chalkboard at school. If Jack multiplied the total sides of the octagon by the total sides of the hexagon and then subtracted the sum of the sides of the pentagon and parallelogram from that, what would be the difference?

Explain: _____

_____

_____

2. Label the decimal points on the number line below.

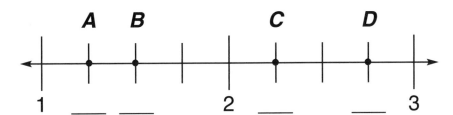

Name _____ **Date** _____

Warm-Up 56

1. Which answer choice below identifies the number line correctly? (*Circle the letter of the correct answer.*)

A. W = 1.3	**B.** W = 1.3	**C.** W = 1.3	**D.** W = 1.3
X = 2.2	X = 2.1	X = 2.3	X = 2.1
Y = 2.5	Y = 2.7	Y = 1.7	Y = 3.4
Z = 3.4	Z = 3.4	Z = 3.4	Z = 2.7

2. Circle the number that has a width of $1\frac{1}{4}$ inches, as shown in the following diagram.

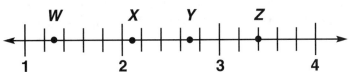

DAILY Warm-Up 57

Name _____ **Date** _____

1. Look at the figure. Which two lines appear to be perpendicular? (*Circle the letter of the correct response.*)

   A. Line *WX* and *ZX*

   B. Line *WX* and *YX*

   C. Line *YZ* and *ZX*

   D. Line *YX* and *YZ*

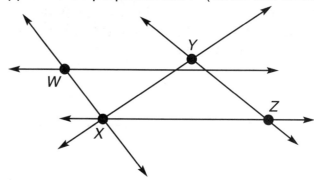

2. Draw a **reflection** of the arrow.

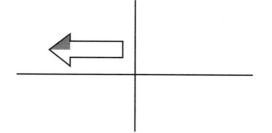

DAILY Warm-Up 58

Name _____ **Date** _____

1. Gisela is making pillows for her couch. She needs 2 feet of lace for each pillow. She plans to make 6 pillows. She can buy the lace in 3-yard, 6-yard, 8-yard, or 10-yard lengths. Which would be the smartest purchase for Gisela to make? (*Circle the letter of the correct response.*)

   A. Buy three 8-yard lengths

   B. Buy two 3-yard lengths

   C. Buy two 10-yard lengths

   D. Buy four 3-yard lengths

2. How many faces does this solid figure have? (*Circle the letter of the correct response.*)

   A. 6

   B. 8

   C. 10

   D. 12

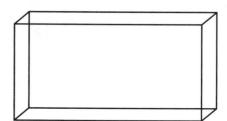

104

Name _____ **Date** _____

1. Which of the following statements is true about an angle? (*Circle the letter of the correct response.*)

   A. An angle is formed when two rays meet at a common endpoint.

   B. An angle is formed when a line segment meets an edge.

   C. An angle is formed by 1 ray.

   D. Not Given

2. Examine the figure below. Are sides *WX* and *YZ* parallel? Circle "Yes" or "No."

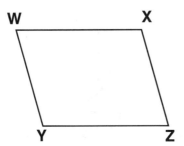

Yes

No

Name _____ **Date** _____

1. Which of the following is true about a hexagon? (*Circle the letter of the true statement.*)

   A. It has 8 sides and 8 vertices.   **C.** It has 5 sides and 5 vertices.

   B. It has 6 sides and 6 vertices.   **D.** It has 4 sides and 4 vertices.

2. Use the chart to find the length of the line segment from start to finish.

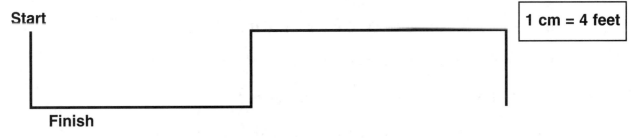

Total Length: _____

DAILY Warm-Up 61 Name _____ Date _____

1. Which object below has one curved surface and two circular bases? (*Circle the letter of the correct object.*)

 **A.**
 B.
 **C.**
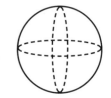 **D.**

2. Use the rectangle below each clock to add 45 minutes to the time shown. The first is done for you.

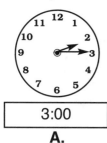
3:00
A.

B.

C.

D.

DAILY Warm-Up 62 Name _____ Date _____

1. Describe how these two shapes are different.

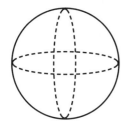 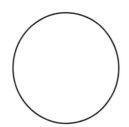

Explain: _____

_____

_____

2. Which statement below is **false**? (*Circle the letter of the false statement.*)

A. A triangular prism has 5 faces, 9 edges, and 6 vertices.

B. A rectangular prism has 6 rectangular faces, 12 edges, and 8 vertices.

C. A cube has 8 vertices, 12 edges, and 6 square faces.

D. A square pyramid has 6 faces, 10 edges, and 5 vertices.

Answer Key

Warm-Up 1
1. The letter A should be circled.
2. B

Warm-Up 2
1. 8 pints
2. C

Warm-Up 3
1. 8 ounces
2. parallel lines

Warm-Up 4
1. 15 ft.
2. B

Warm-Up 5
1. 12 inches
2. C

Warm-Up 6
1. 270 feet
2. C

Warm-Up 7
1. obtuse
2. C

Warm-Up 8
1. 2
2. A

Warm-Up 9
1. C
2. C

Warm-Up 10
1. 5 feet
2. C

Warm-Up 11
1. 2 kilograms
2. A

Warm-Up 12
1. C
2. B

Warm-Up 13
1. A
2. 7 pints

Warm-Up 14
1. B
2. B

Warm-Up 15
1. A
2. B

Warm-Up 16
1. D
2. C

Warm-Up 17
1. 120 inches
2. C

Warm-Up 18
1. B
2. C

Warm-Up 19
1. 1 pound, 8 ounces
2. B

Warm-Up 20
1. C
2. 56 feet

Warm-Up 21
1. C
2. B

Warm-Up 22
1. C
2. B

Warm-Up 23
1. The letter O should be circled.
2. B

Warm-Up 24
1. 2 hours, 45 minutes
2. C

Warm-Up 25
1. B
2. B

Warm-Up 26
1. C
2. D

Warm-Up 27
1. cube or rectangular prism
2. 45 sq. ft.

Warm-Up 28
1. 8 cm
2. 24 cm

Warm-Up 29
1. B
2. C

Warm-Up 30
1. D
2. 2 hours, 30 minutes

Warm-Up 31
1. A
2.

Warm-Up 32
1. B
2. A. face
   B. edge
   C. vertex

Warm-Up 33
1. B
2. A. obtuse
   B. acute
   C. right

Warm-Up 34
1. C
2. obtuse

Warm-Up 35
1. rectangular prism
2. A. True
   B. False
   C. True
   D. False

Warm-Up 36
1. (2, 3)
2. 2

Warm-Up 37
1. 11 cm
2. A

Warm-Up 38
1. 8 cm
2. B

Warm-Up 39
1. C
2. B

Warm-Up 40
1. 300 millimeters
2. B

Warm-Up 41
1. B
2. May

Warm-Up 42
1. A
2. You should convert pounds to ounces. Mike's sister's toy weighs 17 more ounces.

Warm-Up 43
1. 24
2. C

Warm-Up 44
1. 50° F
2. 28 ft.

Warm-Up 45
1. 5 pounds
2. A

Warn-Up 46
1. C
2. 20 millimeters

Warm-Up 47
1. 24 ounces
2. 500 milliliters

Warm-Up 48
1. A
2. 10 feet

Warm-Up 49
1. 24 ounces
2. 60 seconds or 1 minute

Warm-Up 50
1. B
2. 300 square meters

Warm-Up 51
1. C
2. 19 1/2 sq. inches

Warm-Up 52
1. 1 3/4 inches
2. D

Warm-Up 53
1. B
2. D

Warm-Up 54
1. 40 inches
2. B

Warm-Up 55
1. Multiply 8 x 6 = 48. Add 5 and 4 to get 9. Then subtract 48 – 9 = 39.
2. Left to Right: 1.25, 1.5, 2.25, 2.75

Warm-Up 56
1. B
2. The number 1 should be circled.

Warm-Up 57
1. B
2.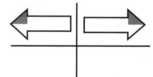

Warm-Up 58
1. B
2. A

Warm-Up 59
1. A
2. Yes

Warm-Up 60
1. B
2. 76 ft.

Warm-Up 61
1. B
2. B. 11:25
   C. 12:45
   D. 2:15

Warm-Up 62
1. One is a solid figure and the other is a plane shape.
2. D

GRAPHS, DATA AND PROBABILITY

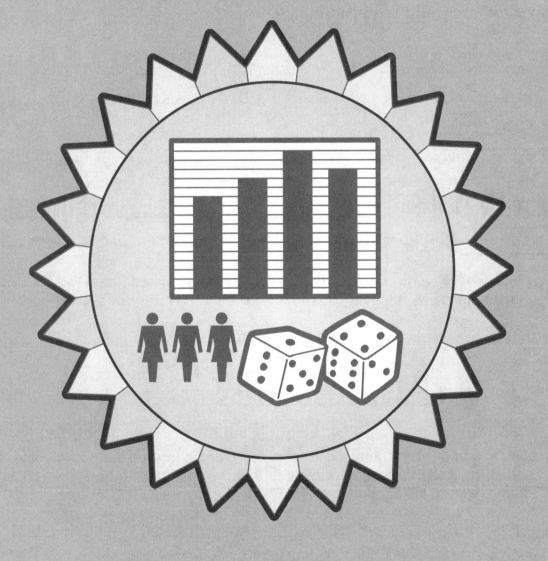

Name _____ **Date** _____

DAILY Warm-Up 1

1. Janice is choosing a shirt to wear. She has 2 red shirts, 1 white shirt, 1 blue shirt, and 3 multicolored shirts. If she chooses a shirt at random, what is the probability she will choose a shirt that is **NOT** white or red? (*Write your answer on the line.*)

_____

2. Ty tossed a quarter 24 times. Which answer is the most likely outcome of his tosses? (*Circle the letter of the correct answer.*)

A. 2 heads in 24 tosses   **C.** 12 heads in 24 tosses

B. 10 heads in 24 tosses   **D.** 24 heads in 24 tosses

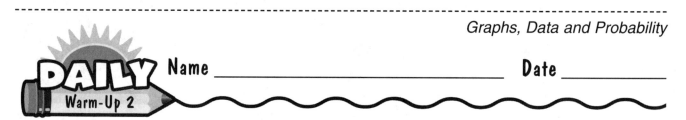

Name _____ **Date** _____

DAILY Warm-Up 2

1. Jeb placed these cards in a bag. If he reaches in and selects 1 card without looking, what is the probability it will be a card with a **D** on it? (*Write your answer on the line.*)

_____

2. Charline has a red scarf, green scarf, pink scarf, and a multicolored scarf in the drawer in her bedroom. If she takes 2 out without looking, which outcome below is **NOT** possible? (*Circle the letter of the correct answer.*)

A. Multicolored and red   **B.** Pink and green   **C.** Green and purple   **D.** Red and pink

DAILY Warm-Up 3

Name _____ Date _____

1. Jason has 6 green toy tractors, 3 red toy tractors, 2 black toy tractors, and 1 brown toy tractor in his toy box. If he reaches in and selects 1 toy tractor without looking, what is the probability that the toy tractor he selects will be red? (*Circle the letter of the correct answer.*)

   A. 2 out of 14   **B.** 1 out of 12   **C.** 3 out of 13   **D.** 3 out of 12

2. Brenda has a blue shirt, a green shirt, and a yellow shirt. She wants to wear one of the shirts with either a black or khaki pair of pants. How many different combinations can she pick from? (*Show your work. Write your final answer on the line.*)

   _____

DAILY Warm-Up 4

Name _____ Date _____

1. Robin has a bag of buttons. The bag contains 2 red buttons, 2 green buttons, and 1 blue button. If Robin took out 2 buttons at a time, which 2 pieces could she **NOT** have taken out? (*Circle the letter of the correct answer.*)

   A. red and blue   **B.** green and red   **C.** red and green   **D.** blue and blue

2. Look at the spinner. If Jacob spins the spinner twice, what are all the possible outcomes? (*Circle the letter of the correct answer.*)

   A. 2 cylinders or 2 cubes

   B. 2 cylinders or 2 cubes or 1 cube and 1 cylinder

   C. 2 cubes or 1 cube and 1 cylinder

   D. 2 cylinders or 1 cube and 1 cylinder

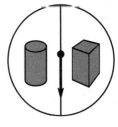

Name _____ **Date** _____

Warm-Up 5

1. James wrote each letter of the name below on different sheets of paper. If he reaches in without looking, what is the probability he will select an A? (*Circle the letter of the correct probability.*)

   A. 2 out of 5   **C.** 1 out of 5

   B. 5 out of 5   **D.** 4 out of 5

AARON

2. Frank twirled the spinner three separate times. What are all the possible color-combination outcomes? (*Write your outcomes on the lines. Note that the order does not matter. For example, yellow-yellow-black is the same as black-yellow-yellow.*)

   _____

   _____

   _____

   _____

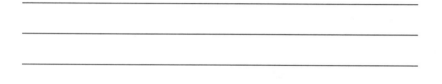

Green | Yellow
Black

Name _____ **Date** _____

Warm-Up 6

1. There are three numbers to Marissa's locker at school. The numbers are 5, 4, and 12. However, she can't remember the order of the numbers. List all the possible combinations for Marissa's locker number.

   _____

   _____

   _____

2. Nancy had 35 yellow hair ribbons. Margaret has 46 yellow ribbons and Sue has 10 fewer yellow ribbons than Margaret. How many ribbons do the girls have altogether? (*Show your work. Write your answer on the line.*)

   _____

1. George is choosing a hat to wear. He has 3 red hats, 2 white hats, 4 blue hats, and 4 green hats. If he chooses a hat at random, what is the probability that he will choose a hat that is **NOT** white or red? (*Write your answer on the line.*)

_____

2. If the arrow is spun once, what is the chance it will land on a Y? (*Circle the letter of the correct answer.*)

A. $\frac{1}{4}$ **C.** $\frac{4}{1}$

B. $\frac{1}{2}$ **D.** $\frac{2}{1}$

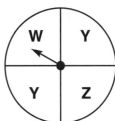

1. Cody flipped a coin 12 times. What is the probability that the coin will land on tails? (*Write your answer on the line.*)

_____

2. Sandra has a deck of cards. From the deck, she took the 3 of clubs, the 7 of diamonds, and the 9 of hearts and placed them side by side on her desk. How many different numbers can she make? (*Write your answer on the line.*)

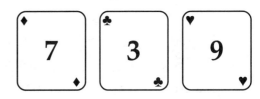

_____

Name _____   **Date** _____

Warm-Up 9

1. Jim is playing a game with his brother. If Jim spins the pointer two times, on what color is Jim most likely to land? On what color is Jim least likely to land? (*Write your answers on the lines.*)

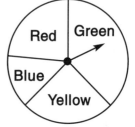

Most Likely: _____

Least Likely:_____

2. What is the largest four-digit even number that has the digits 9, 3, 8, and 4, which are used only once each? (*Write your answer on the line.*)

Name _____   **Date** _____

Warm-Up 10

1. On Friday night, Nathan scored 12 points in a basketball game. His friend Chayanne scored 5 fewer points than Nathan. Daulton scored 9 more points than Chayanne. How many total points did the three boys earn altogether? (*Write your final answer on the lines.*)

_____

2. The bar graph shows the crops grown by members of the Wharton Farmers Association. Use the graph to solve the problems below.

Rice = _____ members

Corn = _____ members

Cotton = _____ members

Soy Beans = _____ members

Maize = _____ members

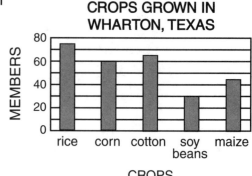

CROPS GROWN IN WHARTON, TEXAS

Name _____ **Date** _____

Warm-Up 11

1. Matthew has three T-shirts hanging in his closet: a red T-shirt, a blue T-shirt, and a white T-shirt. Which combination below is **NOT** possible if Matthew chooses 2 T-shirts from his closet? (*Circle the letter of the correct answer.*)

   A. a white T-shirt and a blue T-shirt

   B. a blue T-shirt and a red T-shirt

   C. a red T-shirt and a green T-shirt

   D. a white T-shirt and a red T-shirt

2. Look at the bar graph. The data represents the number of soft drinks Perry drank during a 5-week period.

   How many soft drinks did Perry drink during the 5-week period?

   _____ soft drinks

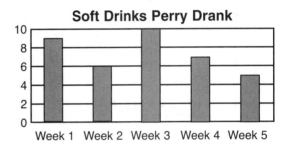

Soft Drinks Perry Drank

Name _____ **Date** _____

Warm-Up 12

1. The table shows the points George scored playing basketball during a 5-day period.

   What is the **median** of the data?

   _____

   How many points did George score on Monday, Wednesday, and Friday?

   _____ points

POINTS SCORED BY GEORGE	
Monday	44
Tuesday	68
Wednesday	62
Thursday	56
Friday	68

2. Candy, Lou, Sam, and Joe are in the same P.E. class at school. They are having a contest to find which person can do the most sit-ups. Joe does 3 fewer sit-ups than Sam. Candy does 20 sit-ups more than Sam. Lou does 10 fewer sit-ups than Joe. Sam does 50 sit-ups. How many sit-ups did each person do? (*Write your answers on the lines.*)

Warm-Up 13

1. Sam, Chuck, and Martin are running a race. How many different ways can they complete the race? (*Fill in the chart.*)

First	Second	Third

2. Juan has a favorite video game. The video game has 20 characters to choose from. Nine of the characters are green, 4 are yellow, 3 are orange, and 4 are red. If Juan picks 1 character to play without looking, what color character will he most likely pick? (*Circle the letter of the correct answer.*)

A. orange character   **B.** yellow character   **C.** red character   **D.** green character

---

Warm-Up 14

1. Deron has a large herd of cattle. Deron's cattle are either black or white. After counting 20 cows, only 2 of these cows were white. After counting another 10 cows, only 1 of these cows was white. Based on this information, which of the following is **most likely**? (*Circle the letter of the best choice.*)

    A. If Deron counts 20 cows, only 1 cow will be black.

    B. If Deron counts 40 cows, about 4 of these cows will be white.

    C. If Deron counts 50 cows, about 5 will be black.

    D. If Deron counts 60 cows, about 1/2 will be white and 1/2 will be black.

2. George made the graph here. If George earned $5 an hour, how much money did George earn in week 4? (*Write your answer on the line.*)

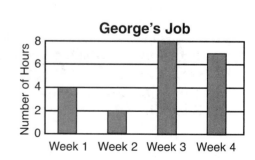

_____

DAILY Warm-Up 15

Name _____ Date _____

1. The graph shows the number of people who received haircuts at Watkins Hair Salon during a 4-day period. At the salon, haircuts cost $5. What is the difference in the amount of money earned on Friday compared to the amount of money earned on Wednesday? (*Write your answer on the line.*)

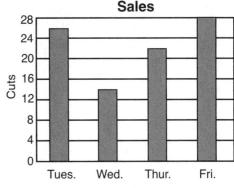

_____

2. If a student spins the pointer twice, what are all the possible outcomes? (*Circle the letter of the correct answer.*)

   A. 2 computers or 2 phones or 1 phone and 2 computers

   B. 2 phones or 2 computers

   C. 2 phones or 1 computer and 1 phone

   D. 2 phones or 2 computers or 1 computer and 1 phone

DAILY Warm-Up 16

Name _____ Date _____

1. Steven went to eat lunch. With his burger, he can choose French fries, curly fries, or tater-tots. Each choice comes with a small, medium, or large drink. From how many different combinations can Steven choose? (*Complete the tree diagram to help find the answer.*)

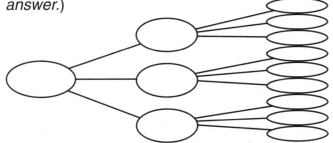

There are_____ combinations.

2. Terry collects hair ribbons. She has 12 more orange hair ribbons than white hair ribbons. She has 3 fewer white hair ribbons than green hair ribbons. She has a total of 8 green hair ribbons. How many hair ribbons of each color does Terry have? (*Write your answers on the lines.*)

   green ribbons: _____   **white ribbons:** _____   **orange ribbons:** _____

Name _____ **Date** _____

Warm-Up 17

1. Lisa keeps pictures of her children on a shelf. The picture of her son Henry is on the left side of Lee. The picture of her daughter Terry is between Henry and Robin. List the order in which the pictures are placed.

_____ _____ _____ _____

2. Cole went to the store and spent half his money. He then spent $10 more on the way home. When he arrived back home, he only had $40. With how much money did Cole have to begin? (*Write your answer on the line.*)

_____

Name _____ **Date** _____

Warm-Up 18

1. Brandi and Maci found 12 shells at the beach altogether. Brandi found 2 more shells than Maci. How many shells did each girl find? (*Write your answers on the lines.*)

Brandi: _____   **Maci:** _____

2. Hank wrote the letters **W**, **X**, **Y**, and **Z** on the board. How many different combinations can you make using these letters? (*Write your final answer on the line.*)

_____

Name _____ **Date** _____

1. Sarah has a bag of buttons. The bag contains 2 purple buttons, 2 white buttons, and 1 black button. If Sarah took out 2 buttons at a time, which 2 pieces could she **NOT** have taken out? (*Circle the letter of the correct answer.*)

A. purple and black   **C.** purple and white

B. white and white   **D.** black and black

2. Terry wrote each letter from her name on index cards and placed them in a bag. If Terry selects one card without looking, what is the probability she will select a card with the letter **R** printed on it? (*Circle the letter of the correct answer.*)

A. $\frac{2}{5}$ **C.** $\frac{1}{5}$

B. $\frac{2}{6}$ **D.** $\frac{1}{2}$

Name _____ **Date** _____

1. Jim has a bag of fishing lures. The bag contains 2 silver lures, 2 yellow lures, and 1 orange lure. If Jim took out 2 fishing lures at a time, which 2 pieces could he **NOT** have taken out? (*Circle the letter of the correct answer.*)

A. silver and orange   **C.** silver and yellow

B. yellow and silver   **D.** orange and orange

2. So far, Stephanie has put five Christmas ornaments on her Christmas tree. The green ornament is at the top of the tree. The gold ornament is lower than the blue ornament and the blue ornament is lower than the green ornament. The silver ornament is lower than the white ornament. Write the order of the placement of ornaments on the tree on the lines below.

DAILY Warm-Up 21

Name _____ Date _____

1. Look at the graph. It shows the number of hours Cody worked during a 4-day period. If he earned $7 an hour, how much money did Cody earn during the 4-day period? (*Write your answer on the line.*)

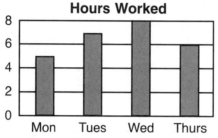

Hours Worked

_____

2. The graph shows the number of ice creams sold during a 4-day period.

   What is the difference between the total ice creams sold on Monday and Wednesday and the total ice creams sold on Tuesday and Thursday?

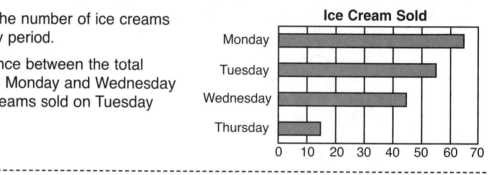

Ice Cream Sold

_____

DAILY Warm-Up 22

Name _____ Date _____

1. What is the probability of spinning a number greater than 7? (*Write your answer on the line.*)

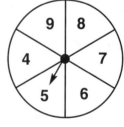

_____

2. Sam has many caps. He has 3 red caps, 1 green cap, 1 yellow cap, and 2 purple caps in his closet. If he chooses a cap at random, what is the probability that he will choose a cap that is **NOT** purple? (*Circle the letter of the correct probability.*)

   A. 2 out of 5   **B.** 4 out of 7   **C.** 1 out of 6   **D.** 5 out of 7

DAILY Warm-Up 23

Name _____ Date _____

1. Look at the pattern of faces. Which number sentence will produce the correct number of faces? (*Circle the letter for the correct answer.*)

A. 3 x 3 =

B. 4 x 3 =

C. 3 x 3 =

D. 6 x 3 =

2. What number is missing in the pattern? (*Write the number in the empty box.*)

33, 27, 21, 15, 9, ☐

DAILY Warm-Up 24

Name _____ Date _____

1. Jeff is playing a number game with his brother. If Jeff spins the pointer, what is the probability it will land on a 3? (*Fill in your answer in the boxes.*)

 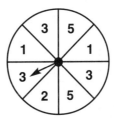

2. The table shows the number of each color necklace Robin has in her jewelry box. If she reaches in without looking, which answer shows the probability of selecting a gold necklace? (*Circle the letter of the correct choice.*)

Color of Necklace	Green	Gold	White	Blue
Number of Necklaces	2	1	4	5

A. $\frac{1}{12}$ **B.** $\frac{2}{12}$ **C.** $\frac{4}{12}$ **D.** $\frac{5}{12}$

Graphs, Data and Probability

Name _____ **Date** _____

1. Look at the pattern of triangles. Which answer will find the total number of triangles? (*Circle the letter of the correct number sentence.*)

A. 16 x 16 =

B. 16 x 3 =

C. 16 x 4 =

D. 16 x 5 =

2. James is playing a game with his son. If he spins the pointer twice, which of these outcomes is possible? (*Circle the letter of the correct answer.*)

A. 2 W's and 2 X's

B. 2 Z's

C. 1 W and 1 Y

D. 2 V's

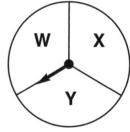

Graphs, Data and Probability

Name _____ **Date** _____

1. Sarah is playing a game with her brother. If she spins the pointer 1 time, what is the probability of landing on the letter **T**? (*Fill in your answer in the boxes.*)

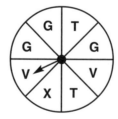

2. Jimmy has 3 green ties, 4 blue ties, 3 yellow ties, and 2 red ties hanging in his closet. If he grabs 1 tie without looking, what is the probability he will select a red tie? (*Circle the letter of the correct answer.*)

A. $\frac{1}{12}$ **B.** $\frac{2}{12}$ **C.** $\frac{4}{12}$ **D.** $\frac{5}{12}$

Name _____ **Date** _____

DAILY Warm-Up 27

1. Hank bought a bag of fishing lures. Of the 15 fishing lures in the bag, 6 are silver, 8 are yellow, and 1 is orange. If Hank picks 2 lures at the same time without looking, what choice below is **NOT** possible? (*Circle the letter of the correct answer.*)

   A. orange and yellow   **C.** yellow and silver

   B. yellow and yellow   **D.** orange and orange

2. What is the possibility of spinning a color other than red, blue, or green? (*Circle the letter of the correct probability.*)

   A. 2 out of 6   **C.** 4 out of 6

   B. 3 out of 6   **D.** 5 out of 6

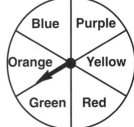

Name _____ **Date** _____

DAILY Warm-Up 28

1. Sam has 6 colored cubes. If Sam picks a cube without looking, what is the probability that he will pick a yellow cube? (*Circle the letter of the correct probability.*)

   A. 2 out of 6
   B. 3 out of 6
   C. 4 out of 6
   D. 5 out of 6

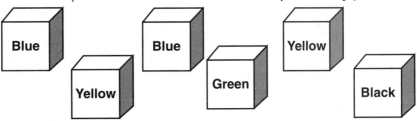

2. Marsha has 3 green shirts, 1 yellow shirt, 2 purple shirts, and 6 orange shirts in her dresser. If she grabs 1 shirt without looking, what color shirt will she most likely pick? (*Circle the letter of the correct answer.*)

   A. green

   B. purple

   C. blue

   D. orange

DAILY Warm-Up 29

Name _____   Date _____

1. Matthew has three T-shirts hanging in his closet: a red T-shirt, a blue T-shirt, and a white T-shirt. Which combination below is possible if Matthew chooses 2 T-shirts from his closet? (*Circle the letter of the correct answer.*)

   A. A white T-shirt and a yellow T-shirt

   B. A blue T-shirt and a red T-shirt

   C. A silver T-shirt and a green T-shirt

   D. A white T-shirt and a black T-shirt

2. Look at the bar graph. The data represents the packs of paper sold during a 5-week period.

   In which 2 weeks were the same number of packs of paper sold?

   Week _____ and Week _____

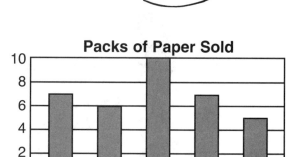

Packs of Paper Sold

DAILY Warm-Up 30

Name _____   Date _____

1. The table shows how many hamburgers were sold each day. Use the table to answer the questions.

   How many more hamburgers were sold on Wednesday and Friday than on Monday and Tuesday?

   _____ hamburgers

Hamburgers Sold During the Week	
Monday	44
Tuesday	68
Wednesday	62
Thursday	56
Friday	68

2. Look at the bar graph. Which statement below is **TRUE**? (*Circle the letter of the true statement.*)

   A. There were more students absent in 4th grade than in 3rd grade.

   B. There were 7 more 2nd graders absent than 5th graders.

   C. The same number of students were absent in the 3rd and 6th grade.

   D. There were 36 students absent altogether.

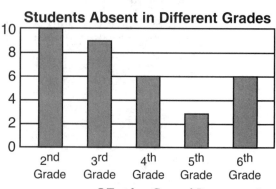

Students Absent in Different Grades

DAILY
Warm-Up 31

Name _____ **Date** _____

1. Look at the graph. Use the information below to complete the graph.

Games Won	
Bears	𝍩𝍩
Tigers	𝍩𝍩𝍩𝍩𝍩𝍩
Colts	𝍩𝍩𝍩𝍩
Cubs	𝍩𝍩𝍩

Games Won During Season

Bears								
Tigers								
Colts								
Cubs								

0   5   10   15   20   25   30   35   40

2. Which spinner has a 50% chance of landing on a number greater than 3? (*Circle the letter of the correct spinner.*)

A.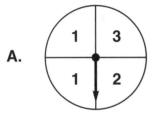
B.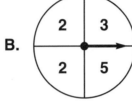
C.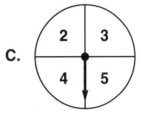
D.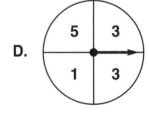

DAILY
Warm-Up 32

Name _____ **Date** _____

1. Marlin has 6 bottles of colored glue. If Marlin grabs 1 bottle of glue without looking, which color glue will he probably pick? (*Circle the letter of the correct answer.*)

A. green

B. red

C. white

D. blue

2. Kelso has 5 green ties, 3 black ties, and 1 brown tie in his closet. If Kelso grabs 2 ties without looking, what color ties are possible? (*Circle the letter of the correct answer.*)

A. 1 yellow tie and 1 brown tie

B. 1 green tie and 1 black tie

C. 1 brown tie and 1 blue tie

D. 1 black tie and 1 red tie

Name _____ **Date** _____

Warm-Up 33

1. Which statement below is **TRUE** about the spinner?
(*Circle the letter of the true statement.*)

   A. It has the best chance of landing on a 3.

   B. It has an equal chance of landing on a 4 or 3.

   C. It will land on a 2.

   D. It has the lowest chance of landing on a 2.

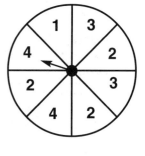

2. If the arrow is spun once, what is the chance it will
land on a **Y**? (*Circle the letter of the correct answer.*)

   A. $\frac{1}{4}$ **C.** $\frac{4}{1}$

   B. $\frac{1}{2}$ **D.** $\frac{2}{1}$

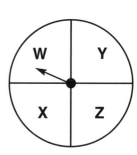

Name _____ **Date** _____

Warm-Up 34

1. Carlos, Nathan, Stephanie, and Sarah were doing a math lesson together. There are
2 parts to the lesson. Two students can pair up on each part. List all the pairs of
students who might work in each group. (*The first combination is listed below.*)

If these students work on **Part 1**	If these students work on **Part 2**
1. Carlos and Nathan	1. Stephanie and Sarah

2. Which spinner has a 75% chance of landing on a number greater than 2 but less
than 6? (*Circle the letter of the correct spinner.*)

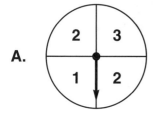

A.   **B.**   **C.**   **D.**

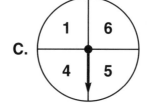

Name _____ **Date** _____

1. What is the probability of landing on a shaded region?
(*Circle the letter of the correct probability.*)

A. $\frac{1}{4}$ C. $\frac{4}{4}$

B. $\frac{8}{5}$ D. $\frac{5}{8}$

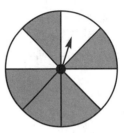

2. Mandy has 3 colored pencils in her backpack: a green pencil, a red pencil, and a blue pencil. Which of the following combinations is **NOT** possible if Mandy chooses 2 pencils from her backpack? (*Circle the letter of the correct answer.*)

A. a green pencil and a blue pencil

B. a red pencil and a blue pencil

C. a yellow pencil and a green pencil

D. a green pencil and a red pencil

Name _____ **Date** _____

1. Circle your answer to the statements below.

A. It is unlikely you will play a video game this year.   **True**   **False**

B. It is likely you will paint your house orange.   **True**   **False**

2. George shuffles the cards below and then lays them face down. If he turns one card over at a time, how many possible combinations can he make? (*Write your final answer on the line.*)

_____

DAILY
Warm-Up 37

Name _____   Date _____

1. Look at the bar graph. When combined, how many more papers did Robin, Heath, and Lee deliver than Terry? (*Write your answer on the line.*)

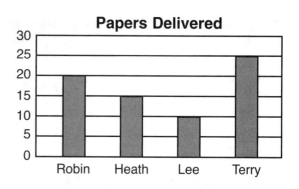

_____

2. Brandi has a blue, a green, a yellow, a red, and an orange crayon sitting on her desk. She asked her friend to follow the clues she gave to find the order of the crayons laid on her desk. The clues are as follows: The color blue is in the middle. The color orange is **NOT** next to the color blue. The color green is last. The color red is between the colors orange and blue. In what order did Brandi use the crayons? (*Label the colors in the crayon diagram below.*)

DAILY
Warm-Up 38

Name _____   Date _____

1. Use the bar graph to solve the problems.

How many more cars were sold during weeks 1, 2, and 4 combined than in week 3?

_____

How many cars were sold altogether?

_____

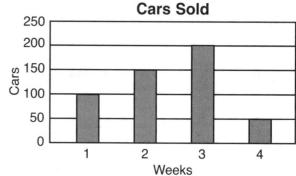

2. The tally chart shows the number of colors of hats Jared sold during January. How many more yellow and orange hats were sold than red and blue hats? (*Write your answer on the line.*)

Jared's Hat Sales During January

Yellow	Purple	Red	Orange	Blue
⳩ℍ ⳩ℍ ⳩ℍ ⳩ℍ	⳩ℍ IIII	⳩ℍ ⳩ℍ II	⳩ℍ ⳩ℍ ⳩ℍ ⳩ℍ	⳩ℍ ⳩ℍ ⳩ℍ II

_____

DAILY
Warm-Up 39

Name _____ **Date** _____

1. Look at the bar graph. How many total fish did George, Hank, and Tammy catch? (*Write your answer on the line.*)

Fish Caught in 1 Month

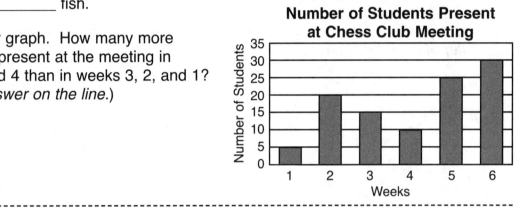

They caught _____ fish.

2. Look at the bar graph. How many more students were present at the meeting in weeks 6, 5, and 4 than in weeks 3, 2, and 1? (*Write your answer on the line.*)

Number of Students Present at Chess Club Meeting

_____

DAILY
Warm-Up 40

Name _____ **Date** _____

1. Jim is playing a game with his sister. It's his turn to roll the die. He wants to roll a 5.

What are all the possible outcomes of Jim's roll?

_____

What is the probability of landing on a 5?

_____

2. The table shows the names Pete wrote down on sheets of paper that he put in a bag. What is the probability of picking a name that starts with the letter **S**? (*Write your answer in the boxes.*)

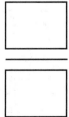

Names		
Stacey	Luke	Margaret
Janet	Roger	Stephanie
Marty	Stan	Sarah

DAILY Warm-Up 41

Name _____ Date _____

1. Wanda wrote these letters on separate cards. She folded them and placed each in a bag. If she reaches in without looking, what is the possibility that she will select a card with a vowel? (*Write your answer in the boxes.*)

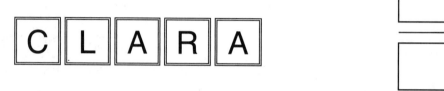

2. Jack spun the pointer one time. How many possible outcomes are there? (*Circle the letter of the correct answer.*)

   A. 6

   B. 10

   C. 9

   D. 8

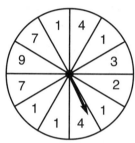

DAILY Warm-Up 42

Name _____ Date _____

1. Sandy bought a bag of candy. There were 12 lemon, 15 grape, 10 chocolate, and 13 strawberry flavored candies in the bag. If Sandy reaches in the bag without looking, what flavor candy will she most likely pick? (*Circle the letter of the correct answer.*)

   A. strawberry   **B.** lemon   **C.** grape   **D.** chocolate

2. Based on the bar graph, which pet was least liked? (*Write your answer on the line.*)

   _____

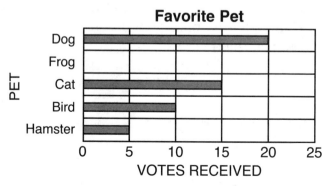

DAILY
Warm-Up 43

Name _____   Date _____

1. Diego went to the music store. The prices, including tax, are sale items shown in the table. Diego bought three items. Diego had $175.00. He bought a CD player, headphones, and a T-shirt. He had enough money to buy 1 more item. What item does Diego have enough money to purchase? (*Write your answer on the line.*)

Mary's Music Store	
CD Player	$85.23
Headphones	$45.93
Portable Stereo	$15.56
Battery Packs	$33.79
Music Videos	$22.13
T-shirts	$24.57

SALE

_____

2. Mary has 20 hair ribbons in a box. Nine of the ribbons are blue, 6 are green, 4 are yellow, and 2 are pink. If she reaches into the box and grabs 1 ribbon without looking, what color ribbon will she least likely pick? (*Circle the letter of the correct answer.*)

A. blue   **B.** green   **C.** yellow   **D.** pink

DAILY
Warm-Up 44

Name _____   Date _____

1. Jennifer bought 3 red cups, 4 blue cups, 6 green cups, 1 yellow cup, and 8 orange cups for her family's camping trip. If she grabs 1 cup without looking, which color cup will she most likely pick? (*Circle the letter of the correct answer.*)

A. blue   **B.** green   **C.** yellow   **D.** orange

2. Courtney, Yesica, Liberty, Marissa, and Essence sit by each other in Mrs. Mann's class. Liberty sits in the middle. Courtney and Marissa sit on the ends. Yesica sits to the right of Liberty. Courtney sits to the right of Yesica. Write the order that they sit. Use their initials in the boxes below.

DAILY Warm-Up 45

Name _____ **Date** _____

1. Hannah bought 1 green flower, 1 red flower, and 1 yellow flower at the store. If she wants to put 3 of the flowers in 1 vase, how many different arrangements of flowers are there for the vase? (*Show your work. Write your final answer on the line.*)

_____

2. Margo has forgotten the combination to her locker at school. The table below shows the combinations she has tried. She knows the numbers to the combination are 4, 8, 9, and 2, but she forgot the order. Which missing combination in the list has she **NOT** tried? (*Write your answer on the line.*)

4892	2894	9842	8294
4829	2849	9824	8249
4298	2498	9248	8492
4289	2489	?	8429
4982	2984	9482	8924
4928	2948	9428	8942

_____

DAILY Warm-Up 46

Name _____ **Date** _____

1. On which spinner will Marsha have the greatest chance of landing on a dog? (*Circle the letter of the correct choice.*)

 A.   B.    C.   D.

2. The bar graph shows the number of stamps in Jeff's stamp collection.

   How many total stamps does Jeff have?

   _____ stamps

   How many more stamps were dated 1957 than 1956 and 1951 combined?

   _____ stamps

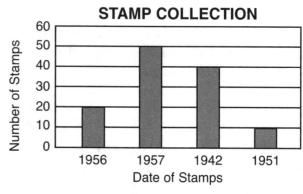

STAMP COLLECTION

DAILY Warm-Up 47   Name _____   Date _____

1. Which spinner gives you the best chance of landing on a number greater than 4 but less than 6? (*Circle the letter of the correct spinner.*)

A. 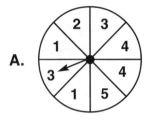   B. 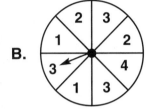   C. 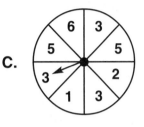   D.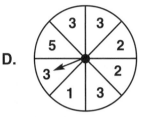

2. Sarah is playing a game with her sister. If Sarah spins the pointer twice, which of these outcomes is possible? (*Circle the letter of the correct choice.*)

   A. 2 blues and 2 whites

   B. 2 yellows

   C. 1 white and 1 red

   D. 2 purples

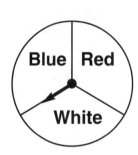

DAILY Warm-Up 48   Name _____   Date _____

1. Look at each spinner. Write the probability of landing on a number greater than 3 but less than 5 for each spinner.

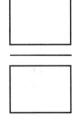 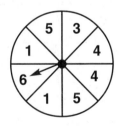   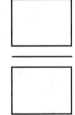 

2. Look at the spinner. What is the likelihood that the spinner will land on a multiple of 3? (*Circle the letter of the best response.*)

   A. Likely   **C.** Possible

   B. Certain   **D.** Impossible

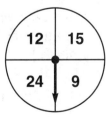

Name _____ **Date** _____

1. Gene bought a bag of lollipops. There were 30 lollipops in the bag. Gene takes the lollipops in groups of 5. How many groups of 5 can Gene make? (*Write your answer on the line.*)

_____

2. Jennifer has 6 pairs (each pair linked together) of gold earrings and 2 pairs (each pair linked together) of silver earrings in her jewelry box. If she grabs 1 pair of earrings without looking, what is the probability it will be a pair of silver earrings?

Explain:_____

_____

_____

Name _____ **Date** _____

1. Cody likes playing with cards. He has two 2 of hearts, two 4 of clubs, two 6 of spades, and three 5 of diamonds. Cody shuffles the cards and places them face down. The pictures below are the cards Cody has already turned over. Based on the pictures, which card will Cody most certainly turn over last? (*Circle the letter of the correct choice.*)

A. 2 of hearts   **B.** 4 of clubs   **C.** 5 of diamonds   **D.** 6 of spades

2. Mark has many T-shirts hanging in his closet. He has 3 red T-shirts, 4 blue T-shirts, 6 green T-shirts, and 8 white T-shirts. If he reaches in his closet and selects 1 T-shirt without looking, what is the probability it will **NOT** be a white T-shirt? (*Circle the letter of the correct probability.*)

A. $\frac{13}{21}$ **B.** $\frac{15}{12}$ **C.** $\frac{8}{21}$ **D.** $\frac{1}{4}$

DAILY Warm-Up 51   Name _____   Date _____

1. Jake has a deck of cards with letters printed on them. He has 2 cards with an A, 2 cards with a B, 2 cards with a C, and 3 cards with a D. If he shuffles the cards and turns them over 1 at a time, what will the last card be? (*Mark the letter on the blank card.*)

| D | B | D | C | A | D | B | C | |

2. Linda has 5 ink pens in her purse. Two are black, 1 is green, and 2 are red. Which of the following combinations is **NOT** possible if Linda chooses 3 ink pens from her purse? (*Circle the letter of the correct answer.*)

A. 2 red and 1 green

B. 1 green and 2 blue

C. 2 black and 1 green

D. 2 red and 1 black

DAILY Warm-Up 52   Name _____   Date _____

1. The table shows how many picture cards Jimmy has. Based on the table, what card will Jimmy most likely turn over next? (*Circle the letter of the correct answer.*)

Cat	2
Dog	3
Rabbit	2
Butterfly	2

A. butterfly   **B.** dog   **C.** cat   **D.** rabbit

2. Sam has 3 blue ties, 2 green ties, 4 multi-colored ties, and 5 black ties in his closet. If he grabs 1 tie without looking, what is the probability he will **NOT** select a multi-colored tie? (*Circle the letter of the correct answer.*)

A. $\frac{2}{14}$ **B.** $\frac{3}{14}$ **C.** $\frac{4}{14}$ **D.** $\frac{10}{14}$

DAILY
Warm-Up 53

Name _____ Date _____

1. Gordon rolled the die below. What is the probability he will get an **even** number? How do you know?

Explain: _____

_____

_____

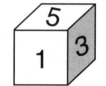

2. What is the probability of spinning a number greater than 3? (*Circle the letter of the correct answer.*)

A. 2 out of 6

B. 3 out of 6

C. 4 out of 6

D. 5 out of 6

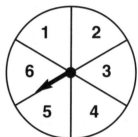

DAILY
Warm-Up 54

Name _____ Date _____

1. Hannah and Heather put their pencils in the same bag. If Hannah grabs 1 pencil without looking, what is the probability she will select a pencil with her name on it? (*Circle the letter of the correct answer.*)

A. 2 out of 6

B. 3 out of 6

C. 4 out of 6

D. 5 out of 6

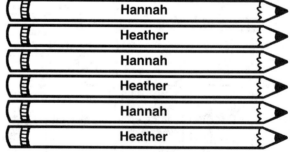

2. Jasper has 3 coins in his pocket: a quarter, a nickel, and a penny. If he grabs 2 coins without looking, what combination of coins is **NOT** possible? (*Circle the letter of the correct answer.*)

A. 2 pennies

B. 1 penny and 1 nickel

C. 1 nickel and 1 quarter

D. 1 quarter and 1 penny

DAILY Warm-Up 55

Name _____   Date _____

1. Look at the bar graph. How many fish
did Lee, Robin, and Terry catch altogether?
(*Write your answer on the line.*)

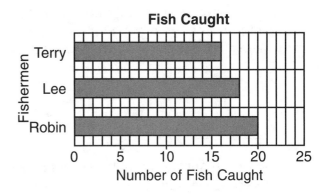

They caught _____ fish.

2. Jane rolled the die one time. What is the probability of rolling an odd number? (*Write
your answer in the boxes.*)

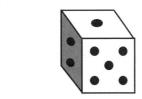

DAILY Warm-Up 56

Name _____   Date _____

1. The bar graph shows the number of tickets
sold by 5 friends. A total of 75 tickets were
sold. Which person sold more than
20 tickets? (*Write your answer on the line.*)

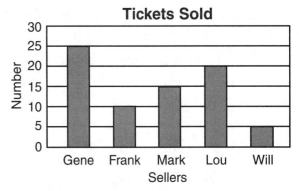

_____

2. The table shows the numbers Pete wrote down on different sheets of paper and then put
into a bag. What is the probability of picking a number greater than 5 but less than 9?
(*Write your answer in the boxes.*)

Numbers		
1	4	7
2	5	8
3	6	9

DAILY Warm-Up 57

Name _____ Date _____

1. Mr. Turner is playing a game with his students. If he spins the pointer 1 time, on what number will the spinner least likely land? (*Write your answer on the line.*)

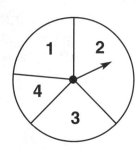

_____

2. The graph shows the number of students who walked home from school over a 5-week period. How many more students walked home in week 3 and week 4 combined than in week 5? (*Write your answer on the line.*)

_____

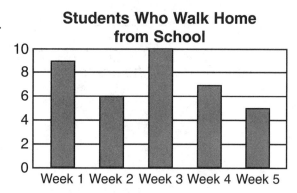

Students Who Walk Home from School

DAILY Warm-Up 58

Name _____ Date _____

1. The table shows the numbers of cans donated during one week.

   How many cans were donated on Monday, Tuesday, and Friday?

   _____

   How many more cans were donated on Thursday than on Tuesday and Wednesday?

   _____

Number of Can Goods Donated	
Monday	112
Tuesday	89
Wednesday	78
Thursday	213
Friday	75

2. Look at the bar graph and answer the questions.

   Which color is least liked?

   _____

   How many votes did the colors blue, red, and green receive?

   _____ votes

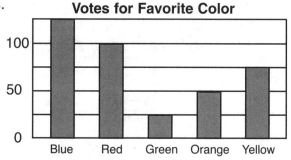

Votes for Favorite Color

DAILY Warm-Up 59

Name _____ Date _____

1. The graph shows the number of students who ride their bikes to and from school.

How many students rode their bikes on Monday and Wednesday combined?

_____

Which day do you think the weather was bad?

_____

Number of Bike Riders

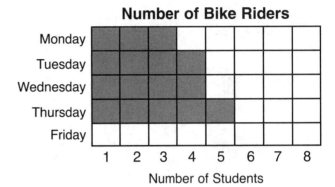

Number of Students

2. Look at the spinner. On what number will the spinner least likely land? (*Circle the letter of the correct answer.*)

A. 6

C. 4

B. 5

D. 3

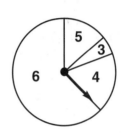

DAILY Warm-Up 60

Name _____ Date _____

1. Look at the spinner. What is the probability of landing on a multiple of 3? (*Circle the letter of the correct answer.*)

A. Likely

B. Unlikely

C. Certain

D. Impossible

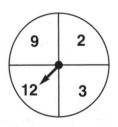

2. The graph shows the number of hours four teachers worked on their computers over a 1-week period. Mrs. Right worked 15 hours and Mrs. Winston worked 20 hours. How many hours did Mr. Hanks work? (*Write your answer on the line.*)

_____

Hours Worked on Computers	
Mr. Winston	🖥 🖥 🖥 🖥
Mrs. Right	🖥 🖥 🖥
Mr. Hanks	🖥 🖥 🖥 🖥 🖥 🖥
Mrs. Higgs	🖥

Name _____ **Date** _____

1. On what animal will the spinner most likely land?
(*Circle the letter of the best answer.*)

A.   C.

B.   D.

2. Use the graph to answer the question.

If Jody rode 30 miles and Sarah rode 40 miles, how many miles did Scott ride? (*Write your answer on the line.*)

_____

Miles Ridden on Bike	
Jody	🚲 🚲 🚲
Scott	🚲 🚲
Cassidy	🚲
Sarah	🚲 🚲 🚲 🚲

Name _____ **Date** _____

1. Use the bar graph to answer the questions below.

How many more subscriptions must Harry sell to match the subscriptions Kaylee sold?

_____

How many subscriptions were sold altogether?

_____

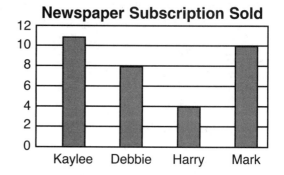

Newspaper Subscription Sold

2. Maria has 2 gold hair ribbons, 3 green hair ribbons, 4 yellow hair ribbons, and 1 blue hair ribbon in her drawer. If she grabs one hair ribbon without looking, which color will she most likely pick? (*Circle the letter of the correct color.*)

A gold   **B.** green   **C.** yellow   **D.** blue

Answer Key

Warm-Up 1
1. 4/7 or 4 out of 7
2. C

Warm-Up 2
1. 2/5 or 2 out of 5
2. C

Warm-Up 3
1. D
2. 6 combinations

Warm-Up 4
1. D
2. B

Warm-Up 5
1. A
2. green, green, green
   green, green, black
   green, green, yellow
   green, black, yellow
   black, black, black
   black, black, green
   black, black, yellow
   yellow, yellow, yellow
   yellow, yellow, black
   yellow, yellow, green

Warm-Up 6
1. 5, 4, and 12
   5, 12, and 4
   4, 5, and 12
   4, 12, and 5
   12, 4, and 5
   12, 5, and 4
2. 117 ribbons

Warm-Up 7
1. 8/13 or 8 out of 13
2. B

Warm-Up 8
1. 1/2
2. 6

Warm-Up 9
1. Most Likely: Green
   Least Likely: Blue
2. 9834

Warm-Up 10
1. 35 points
2. Rice = 75 members
   Corn = 60 members
   Cotton = 65 members
   Soy Beans = 30 members
   Maize = 45 members

Warm-Up 11
1. C
2. 37

Warm-Up 12
1. 62; 174
2. Candy = 70
   Lou = 37
   Sam = 50
   Joe = 47

Warm-Up 13
1.

First	Second	Third
Sam	Chuck	Martin
Sam	Martin	Chuck
Chuck	Sam	Martin
Chuck	Martin	Sam
Martin	Sam	Chuck
Martin	Chuck	Sam

2. D

Warm-Up 14
1. B
2. $35

Warm-Up 15
1. $70
2. D

Warm-Up 16
1. 9
2. green ribbons = 8
   white ribbons = 5
   orange ribbons = 17

Warm-Up 17
1. Left to Right: Robin, Terry, Henry, Lee
2. $100

Warm-Up 18
1. Brandi: 7 shells
   Maci: 5 shells
2. 24 combinations

Warm-Up 19
1. D
2. A

Warm-Up 20
1. D
2.

Warm-Up 21
1. $182
2. 40

Warm-Up 22
1. 2 out of 6 or 2/6; 1 out of 3 or 1/3
2. D

Warm-Up 23
1. D
2. 3

Warm-Up 24
1. 3/8
2. A

Warm-Up 25
1. B
2. C

Warm-Up 26
1. 2/8
2. B

Warm-Up 27
1. D
2. B

Warm-Up 28
1. A
2. D

Warm-Up 29
1. B
2. Week 1 and Week 4

Warm-Up 30
1. 18
2. B

Warm-Up 31

1.

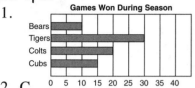

Games Won During Season

Bears
Tigers
Colts
Cubs

0 5 10 15 20 25 30 35 40

2. C

Warm-Up 32

1. D
2. B

Warm-Up 33

1. B
2. A

Warm-Up 34

1. If these students work on Part 1:
   1. Carlos and Nathan
   2. Carlos and Stephanie
   3. Carlos and Sarah
   4. Nathan and Stephanie
   5. Nathan and Sarah
   6. Stephanie and Sarah

   Then these students will work on Part 2:
   1. Stephanie and Sarah
   2. Nathan and Sarah
   3. Nathan and Stephanie
   4. Carlos and Sarah
   5. Carlos and Stephanie
   6. Carlos and Nathan
2. B

Warm-Up 35

1. D   2. C

Warm-Up 36

1. A. False
   B. False
2. 6

Warm-Up 37

1. 20
2. Left to Right: Orange, Red, Blue, Yellow, Green

Warm-Up 38

1. 100; 500
2. 11

Warm-Up 39

1. 75
2. 25 more students

Warm-Up 40

1. 1, 2, 3, 4, 5, 6
   1 out of 6 or 1/6
2. 4/9

Warm-Up 41

1. 2/5
2. A

Warm-Up 42

1. C
2. frog

Warm-Up 43

1. Portable Stereo
2. D

Warm-Up 44

1. D
2. Left to Right: Marissa, Essence, Liberty, Yesica, Courtney

Warm-Up 45

1. 6 arrangements
2. 9284

Warm-Up 46

1. C
2. 120; 20

Warm-Up 47

1. C
2. C

Warm-Up 48

1. 2/8, 1/8
2. B

Warm-Up 49

1. 6 groups
2. Jennifer has a 2 out of 8 (2/8) chance of picking a linked pair of silver earrings.

Warm-Up 50

1. C
2. A

Warm-Up 51

1. A
2. B

Warm-Up 52

1. B
2. D

Warm-Up 53

1. Gordon has a 3 out of 6 (3/6) chance of rolling an even number. The numbers on the die are 1, 2, 3, 4, 5, and 6. Only 3 of these numbers are even.
2. B

Warm-Up 54

1. B
2. A

Warm-Up 55

1. 54
2. 3/6 or 1/2

Warm-Up 56

1. Gene
2. 3/9 or 1/3

Warm-Up 57

1. 4
2. 12 more students

Warm-Up 58

1. 276 cans, 46
2. green, 250

Warm-Up 59

1. 7, Friday
2. D

Warm-Up 60

1. A
2. 30 hours

Warm-Up 61

1. C
2. 15 miles

Warm-Up 62

1. 7; 33
2. C

ALGEBRA, PATTERNS AND FUNCTIONS

DAILY Warm-Up 1

Name _____   **Date** _____

1. The table shows the total miles Robin drove her daughter to dance practice after different numbers of days. If the pattern continues, how many miles will Robin have driven her daughter after 21 days? (*Write your answer on the line.*)

Number of Days	Number of Miles
2	28
5	70
8	112

_____

2. Look at the table below. Based on the number pattern shown in the table, how many shots will Jack make in 25 minutes? (*Circle the letter of the correct choice.*)

   A. 140 shots

   B. 120 shots

   C. 100 shots

   D. 80 shots

Jack's Basketball Results			
Number of Minutes	5	10	15
Number of Shots Made	20	40	60

DAILY Warm-Up 2

Name _____   **Date** _____

1. Ms. Hargrove walks for exercise. The table shows the total miles she walks after different numbers of days. If the pattern continues, how many miles will Ms. Hargrove have walked after 13 days? (*Write your answer on the line.*)

Number of Days	Number of Miles walked
1	5
5	25
9	45

_____

2. The bar graph shows the number of laps 4 friends run each week. Which two friends ran a total of 14 laps combined? (*Circle the letter of the correct response.*)

   A. Ken and Tom

   B. Sam and Ken

   C. Jon and Tom

   D. Sam and Tom

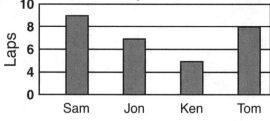

Name _____ **Date** _____

DAILY Warm-Up 3

1. Jack drew this pattern on the chalkboard at school. Based on the pattern, which geometric shape would Jack draw next? (*Circle the letter of the correct shape.*)

A. (octagon)   B. (triangle)   C. (right triangle)   D. (inverted triangle)

2. What happens to the number in the "IN" column to get the number in the "OUT" column? (*Write the answer on the lines.*)

IN	OUT
2	8
4	16
6	24
8	32

_____

_____

_____

Name _____ **Date** _____

DAILY Warm-Up 4

1. Sam plays basketball at school. For each basket (2 points each) Sam scores in a game, his dad promised him $5. In the first game of the season, Sam scored 24 points earning $60 from his dad. In the second game, Sam scored 16 points earning $40 from his dad. Based on the pattern, if Sam scored 56 points in the third game, how much money can he expect to receive from his dad? (*Write the answer on the line.*)

_____

2. What happens to the number in the "IN" column to get the number in the "OUT" column? (*Circle the letter of the correct response.*)

A. It has 8 subtracted from it.

B. It is multiplied by 5.

C. It is divided by 5.

D. It has 5 added to it.

IN	OUT
10	2
15	3
20	4
25	5

DAILY
Warm-Up 5

Name _____ Date _____

1. The table below shows the number of cans Mary recycled for a project at school. If the pattern continues, how many cans will she have recycled after 10 weeks? *(Write your answer on the line.)*

IN	OUT
2	8
4	16
6	24
8	32

_____

2. Look at the table to the right. If the pattern continues, what would be the "OUT" number if 14 is put in the "IN" column? *(Write the answer on the line.)*

IN	OUT
2	8
4	16
6	24
8	32
10	40
12	48

_____

DAILY
Warm-Up 6

Name _____ Date _____

1. Jackie arranged her cards in the pattern below. Which number sentence best represents Jackie's pattern? *(Circle the correct letter choice.)*

   A. 10 + 3 = 13

   B. 10 + 10 = 20

   C. 10 x 3 = 30

   D. 10 + 4 = 14

2. Which answer choice describes the rule for the pattern of numbers below? *(Circle the letter of the correct choice.)*

   A. add 5, subtract 3

   B. add 5, subtract 2

   C. add 5, subtract 4

   D. add 5, divide by 4

5	10	6	11	7

1. If the pattern continues, which answer choice shows the correct number of squares that will be next in the pattern? (*Circle the letter of the correct choice.*)

A. 66

B. 57

C. 52

D. 45

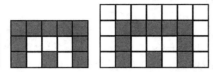 

_____

2. Mr. Clay wrote the numbers 1, 4, 8, 13, and 19 on the board. If he continues the pattern, what are the next four numbers in his pattern? (*Write the answers on the line.*)

_____, _____, _____, _____

1. On Monday, Hunter received $2 from his aunt. Every day after that, he received 3 times as much as he did the day before. If this pattern continues, how much money will Hunter receive on Friday? (*Circle the letter of the correct amount.*)

A. $6

B. $18

C. $54

D. $162

2. Jack drew this pattern of dots on the board. If he continues the pattern one more time, how many dots will be in the next figure of the pattern? (*Write the answer on the line.*)

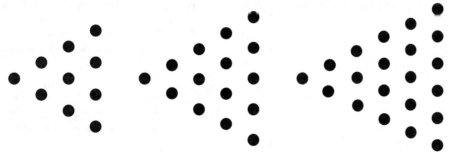

_____

1. Solve for **y**.

$$y - 1,904 = 2,485$$

$$y = \underline{\hspace{3cm}}$$

2. Mrs. Clark wrote the table of ordered pairs below on the chalkboard. She asked her students to find what happens to the numbers in **COLUMN D** to get the numbers in **COLUMN E**. (*Circle the letter of the correct explanation.*)

A. Each number in COLUMN D is 12 more than its pair in COLUMN E.

B. Each number in COLUMN E is 12 less than its pair in COLUMN D.

C. To get each number in COLUMN E, divide its pair in COLUMN D by 12.

D. Each number in COLUMN E is 20 more than its pair in COLUMN D.

COLUMN D	COLUMN E
144	12
132	11
126	10
108	9
96	8
84	7

1. What are the next three numbers in the pattern? (*Write them on the lines.*)

14, 28, 42, 56, _____, _____, _____

2. Thirty customers came into Bullet's Bargain Basement on Monday. On Tuesday, 60 people entered. On Wednesday, 90 people entered the store. If this pattern continues, how many customers could the store expect to enter on Friday? (*Write the answer on the line.*)

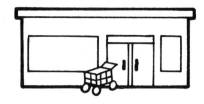

_____

Name _____ **Date** _____

1. Jefferson practiced his multiplication facts for 15 minutes on Monday, 15 minutes on Tuesday, 15 minutes on Wednesday, and 15 minutes on Thursday. If Jefferson continues this pattern of practice, how many days will it take him to get in 2 hours of multiplication practice? (*Write the answer on the line.*)

_____

2. Fill in the missing numbers to complete the pattern.

20, 20, 20, 1, 2, 3, 19, 19, 19, 4, 5, 6, 18, 18, _____, _____, _____

Name _____ **Date** _____

1. What are the next three numbers in the pattern?

18, 23, 27, 32, _____ , _____ , _____

2. Solve for *y*.

$$2,045 + y = 4,503$$

$$y = _____$$

DAILY
Warm-Up 13

Name _____   Date _____

1. Travis arranged some cubes in the pattern below. Which number sentence best represents Travis' pattern? (*Circle the letter of the correct response.*)

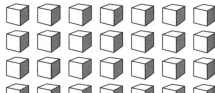

   A. 6 x 5 = 30   **C.** 7 x 7 = 49

   B. 6 x 7 = 42   **D.** 7 x 8 = 56

2. The number sentences below are both true. Which of the following equations must also be true? (*Circle the letter of the correct response.*)

DAILY
Warm-Up 14

Name _____   Date _____

1. Mrs. Morgan asked her students to count to 60 using multiples of 6. If her class did this correctly, which answer choice below is true about their response? (*Circle the letter of the correct choice.*)

   A. They are odd numbers.   **C.** They are all two-digit numbers.

   B. They all can be divided by 3.   **D.** Not given

2. Jennifer had 12 yellow buttons, 14 green buttons, 9 silver buttons, 18 red buttons, and some blue buttons. Altogether she had 67 buttons. How many blue buttons did she have? (*Write your answer on the line.*)

_____

Name _____ **Date** _____

1. Look at the pattern. If the pattern continues, what will be the next two numbers? (Circle the letter of the correct choice.)

A. 9 and 10

B. 10 and 11

C. 10 and 12

D. 11 and 12

6, 8, 7, 9, 8, 10, 9, 11, _____ , _____

2. Look at the model below. If the number 6 is put in the "IN" side, what would be the number that comes out the "OUT" side?

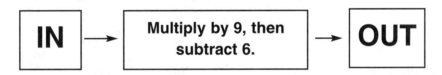

IN → Multiply by 9, then subtract 6. → OUT

_____

Name _____ **Date** _____

1. Cindy rides the bus home from work each day. The schedule below shows the time each bus arrives at the bus stop. Cindy missed the 7:30 bus. How many minutes will Cindy have to wait for the next bus? (*Circle the letter of the correct answer.*)

BUS SCHEDULE
7:15   7:30   7:45   8:00

A. 25 minutes   **B.** 20 minutes   **C.** 15 minutes   **D.** 10 minutes

2. Solve the problem below.

IN	0	1	2	3	4	5
OUT	3	4	5	6	7	8

If the pattern of numbers continues, what would be the "OUT" number if 12 is put in the "IN" column?

_____

DAILY
Warm-Up 17

Name _____

Date _____

1. How many times does the number 5 appear in the numbers 1 to 100? (*Finish filling out the hundreds chart to help find the answer. Write the final answer on the line.*)

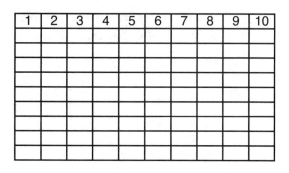

1	2	3	4	5	6	7	8	9	10

_____

2. Which answer choice describes the rule for the pattern of numbers below? (*Circle the letter of the correct choice.*)

| 27 | 36 | 32 | 41 | 37 |

A. add 4, subtract 9

C. add 9, subtract 4

B. multiply 9, subtract 4

D. multiply 4, subtract 9

DAILY
Warm-Up 18

Name _____

Date _____

1. Jillian wrote the numbers 1, 2, 4, 7, and 11 on the board. If she continues the pattern, what are the next four numbers in her pattern? (*Write the answers on the lines.*)

_____, _____, _____, _____

2. Each day, Mr. Pate eats two donuts. Which number sentence shows the number of days it will take Mr. Pate to eat a dozen donuts? (*Circle the letter of the correct response.*)

A. 12 ÷ 2 = ☐

C. 12 + 2 = ☐

B. 12 x 2 = ☐

D. 12 − 2 = ☐

Name _____ **Date** _____

1. The "IN" numbers have been changed by a rule into "OUT" numbers. What is the rule? (*Circle the letter of the correct choice.*)

A. subtract 10

B. add 10

C. divide by 5

D. multiply by 10

IN	OUT
50	10
40	8
30	6
20	4

2. A family donates 3 bags of groceries to charity every 2 months. How many months would it take them to donate a total of 15 bags of groceries? (*Write the answer on the line.*)

_____

Name _____ **Date** _____

Warm-Up 20

1. Jill is driving across Texas to see her grandmother. For every 4 hours she drives, she stops 2 times. How many times will Jill stop if she drives 14 hours? (*Write the answer on the line.*)

_____

2. Jason loves to play basketball. Jason practices his 3-point shot every day. For every 12 shots he makes, he misses 2. How many shots can Jason expect to miss if he shoots a total of 60 times? (*Write the answer on the line.*)

_____

DAILY **Warm-Up 21**

1. Jackie arranged her cards in the pattern below. Which number sentence best represents Jackie's pattern? (*Circle the letter of the correct choice.*)

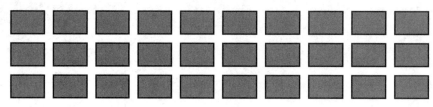

A. 10 + 3 = 13   **B.** 10 + 10 = 20   **C.** 10 x 3 = 30   **D.** 10 + 4 = 14

2. Which answer choice describes the rule for the pattern on numbers below? (*Circle the letter of the correct choice.*)

3	9	6	12	9

A. add 6, subtract 5   **B.** add 3, subtract 6   **C.** add 6, subtract 3   **D.** add 4, subtract 2

DAILY **Warm-Up 22**

1. Describe the pattern.

_____

_____

_____

IN	OUT
2	10
5	13
8	16
11	19
14	22

2. What happens to the number in the "IN" column to get the number in the "OUT" column? (*Circle the letter of the correct answer.*)

A. It has 3 subtracted from it.

B. It has 3 added to it.

C. It is multiplied by 3.

D. It is divided by 3.

IN	OUT
3	9
4	12
5	15
6	18

Name _____ **Date** _____

Warm-Up 23

1. Tanya and her brothers and sister went Easter egg hunting. Tanya found 3 more eggs than Rebecca. Rebecca found 5 more eggs than Logan. Logan found 3 more eggs than Harold. Harold found 13 eggs. Fill out the table to show how many Easter eggs each person found.

Name	Logan	Tanya	Harold	Rebecca
Number of Eggs			13	

2. Jimmy caught 10 more fish than Frank. Which of the choices below shows the number of fish that Jimmy and Frank could have caught? (*Circle the letter of the correct choice.*)

A. Jimmy 10, Frank 2

C. Frank 18, Jimmy 35

B. Jimmy 10, Frank 22

D. Frank 5, Jimmy 15

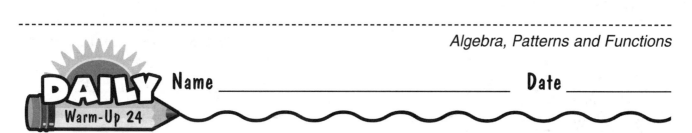

Name _____ **Date** _____

Warm-Up 24

1. Sandy is making cupcakes. For every 4 chocolate cupcakes she makes, she also makes 7 strawberry cupcakes. If Sandy makes a total of 28 strawberry cupcakes, how many chocolate cupcakes will she make? (*Write your answer on the line.*)

_____

2. For every small seashell Nancy found at the beach, she also found 5 large seashells. If Nancy found a total of 20 large seashells, how many small seashells did she find? (*Circle the letter of the correct answer.*)

A. 5

B. 4

C. 3

D. 2

Name _____ **Date** _____

Warm-Up 25

1. Jack drew a number of arrows. How many arrows did Jack draw? (*Write your answer on the line.*)

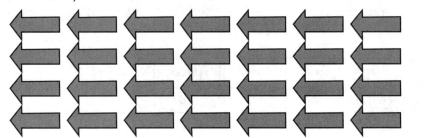

_____

2. Sarah has a fish store. The table below shows the number of fish placed in different numbers of fish tanks. According to the table, how many fish are in 5 fish tanks? (*Circle the letter of the correct answer.*)

A. 45

B. 48

C. 63

D. 81

Number of Fish	Number of Fish Tanks
36	4
54	6
72	8
90	10

Name _____ **Date** _____

Warm-Up 26

1. Hank and Mark run laps around the school track each day. For every 2 laps Hank runs, Mark runs 4. If Mark ran a total of 16 laps, how many laps did Hank run? (*Write your answer on the line.*)

_____

2. What number belongs in the box? (*Circle the letter of the correct response.*)

A. 6

B. 7

C. 8

D. 9

$$45 \div \boxed{} = 5$$

DAILY Warm-Up 27

Name _____ Date _____

1. The table below shows the number of laps Mark swam on different numbers of days. What expression can be used to find how many laps Mark will swim after 9 days? (*Circle the letter of the correct response.*)

A. $9 \times 3 =$

B. $9 \times 4 =$

C. $9 \times 5 =$

D. $9 \times 6 =$

Number of Days	Number of Laps
2	8
4	16
6	24
8	32

2. Look at the equations below. Fill in the missing numbers.

$$3 \times \boxed{} = 27 \qquad 27 \div \boxed{} = 9$$

$$9 \times \boxed{} = 27 \qquad 27 \div \boxed{} = 3$$

DAILY Warm-Up 28

Name _____ Date _____

1. Look at the table. Explain how to find the number of candy bars in 7 boxes.

_____

_____

_____

Number of Boxes	Number of Candy Bars
2	8
4	16
6	24
8	32

2. Which answer choice describes the rule for the pattern of numbers below? (*Circle the letter of the correct rule.*)

A. add 5, add 10

B. subtract 5, add 10

C. subtract 5, add 20

D. subtract 5, subtract 10

| 15 | 10 | 20 | 15 | 25 |

DAILY
Warm-Up 29

Name _____ Date _____

1. Linda wants to give 4 pieces of candy to each of her friends. Which table shows the total amount of candy Linda will need for different numbers of friends? (*Circle the letter of the correct table.*)

A.

# of Friends	Candies Needed
1	5
2	6
3	7
4	8

B.

# of Friends	Candies Needed
4	16
5	20
6	24
7	28

C.

# of Friends	Candies Needed
12	8
13	9
14	10
15	11

D.

# of Friends	Candies Needed
16	4
20	5
24	6
28	7

2. Look at the table. How many paintbrushes are in 8 packages? (*Write your answer on the line.*)

Number of Packages	1	2	3	4	5	6	7	8
Number of Paintbrushes	2	4	6	8	10	12	14	

There are _____ paintbrushes in 8 packages.

DAILY
Warm-Up 30

Name _____ Date _____

1. The table shows the number of crayons in different numbers of boxes. How many crayons are in 4 boxes? (*Write your answer on the line.*)

Number of Boxes	Number of Crayons
1	5
3	15
5	25
7	35
8	40

_____

2. Write four correct number sentences below for the numbers 24, 6, and 4.

_____ X _____ = _____   _____ ÷ _____ = _____

_____ X _____ = _____   _____ ÷ _____ = _____

Name _____ Date _____

DAILY Warm-Up 31

1. Marco loves his new video game. For each level he advances in the game, he receives 2,000 points. Based on the pattern, how many points will Marco have if he has advanced to the fifth level? (*Write the answer on the line.*)

_____

2. Solve the problems below.

$54 \div \underline{\hspace{1cm}} = 6$ $54 \div \underline{\hspace{1cm}} = 9$ $40 \div \underline{\hspace{1cm}} = 8$

$\underline{\hspace{1cm}} \times 9 = 45$ $36 \div \underline{\hspace{1cm}} = 4$ $\underline{\hspace{1cm}} \times 7 = 42$

$81 \div \underline{\hspace{1cm}} = 9$ $36 \div \underline{\hspace{1cm}} = 6$ $28 \div \underline{\hspace{1cm}} = 4$

Name _____ Date _____

DAILY Warm-Up 32

1. What letters go next in the pattern? (*Circle the letter for the correct response.*)

| A, A, B, B, C, _____ , _____ |

A. B and C   **B.** C and D   **C.** D and D   **D.** E and E

2. Sue built a magic number machine for her class. For each number she placed in the machine, a different number came out. The table shows the numbers Sue has already put in the machine. Based on the table, if Sue puts the number 7 in the "IN" side, what number will come out the "OUT" side? (*Write the answer on the line.*)

IN	OUT
5	40
6	48
7	
8	64

_____

DAILY **Warm-Up 33**

Name _____ Date _____

1. What should you do to find the next number in the pattern? (*Circle the letter of the correct answer.*)

A. add 9 to 158

B. add 10 to 158

C. subtract 10 from 158

D. subtract 10 from 188

$$188, 178, 168, 158, \underline{\hspace{1.5cm}}$$

2. Solve the problems below.

$(2 \times 4) \div 4 = \underline{\hspace{1cm}}$ $(6 \times 4) \div 3 = \underline{\hspace{1cm}}$ $(7 \times 2) \div 2 = \underline{\hspace{1cm}}$

$(8 \div 4) \times 3 = \underline{\hspace{1cm}}$ $(12 \div 4) \times 2 = \underline{\hspace{1cm}}$ $(10 \div 2) \times 3 = \underline{\hspace{1cm}}$

$3 \times (15 \div 3) = \underline{\hspace{1cm}}$ $3 \times (4 \div 4) = \underline{\hspace{1cm}}$ $9 \times (15 \div 3) = \underline{\hspace{1cm}}$

- -

DAILY **Warm-Up 34**

Name _____ Date _____

1. Dahlia folded her green, yellow, orange, and white T-shirts and placed them in her drawer. The green was on the top of the white T-shirt. The orange was on top of all other T-shirts. The yellow shirt was on top of the green shirt but under the orange shirt. List the order Dahlia placed her T-shirts in her drawer.

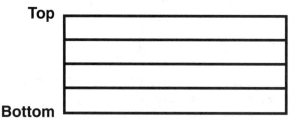

Top

Bottom

2. Solve the problems below.

$(7 \times 4) \div 4 = \underline{\hspace{1cm}}$ $(2 \times 2) \div 2 = \underline{\hspace{1cm}}$ $(2 \times 4) \div 4 = \underline{\hspace{1cm}}$

$(9 \div 3) \times 8 = \underline{\hspace{1cm}}$ $(12 \div 4) \times 3 = \underline{\hspace{1cm}}$ $(8 \div 4) \times 3 = \underline{\hspace{1cm}}$

$3 \times (18 \div 2) = \underline{\hspace{1cm}}$ $3 \times (21 \div 3) = \underline{\hspace{1cm}}$ $5 \times (15 \div 5) = \underline{\hspace{1cm}}$

DAILY
Warm-Up 35

Name _____   **Date** _____

1. Liz bought two gifts for her brother. The larger gift weighed 6 pounds more than the smaller gift. If the smaller gift weighed 5 pounds, how many pounds did the larger gift weigh? (*Write the answer on the line.*)

_____

2. Look at the table. Fill the missing numbers on the table, and then explain the rule that helped you complete the table.

Explain: _____

_____

_____

IN	OUT
2	4
3	5
4	6

DAILY
Warm-Up 36

Name _____   **Date** _____

1. Look at the pattern. How many blocks will it take to make the next figure in the pattern? (*Circle the letter of the correct answer.*)

   A. 11

   B. 12

   C. 13

   D. 14

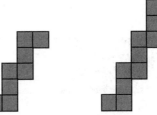

_____

2. Walter wrote the numbers 2, 4, and 9 on the board. If Walter wants to make a three-digit number using the three numbers he wrote on the board, how many different combinations can he make? (*Write the answer on the line.*)

_____

DAILY
Warm-Up 37

Name _____ Date _____

1. Look at the pattern of shapes below. Draw the next two shapes.

2. The table below shows the cost of different numbers of balloons at a store. Based on the pattern in the table, what is the cost of two balloons? (*Write your answer on the line.*)

Number of Balloons	Cost
1	$0.15
3	$0.45
5	$0.75
7	$1.05

_____

DAILY
Warm-Up 38

Name _____ Date _____

1. The table below shows the number of aluminum cans 4 friends collected. Each friend, except Dan, wrote down the number of cans he collected. They know they collected a total of 385 cans. How many cans did Dan collect? (*Fill in the answer on the table.*)

Number of Cans	120	103		99
Name	Mark	Jim	Dan	Sam

2. Solve the problems below.

$(4 \times 4) + 6 =$ _____ $(8 \times 6) + 3 =$ _____

$9 - (12 \div 6) =$ _____ $14 + (21 \div 7) =$ _____

Name _____   **Date** _____

1. Which number sentence is in the same fact family as 56 ÷ 7 = 8? (*Circle the letter of the correct answer.*)

A. 8 + ___ = 5   **B.** ___ − 8 = 5   **C.** 7 x ___ = 56   **D.** 56 x 7 = ___

2. In which number sentence does 5 make the equation true? (*Circle the letter of the correct answer.*)

A. 40 ÷ 4 = ☐   **B.** 36 ÷ 6 = ☐   **C.** 20 ÷ 4 = ☐   **D.** 24 ÷ 6 = ☐

- -

Name _____   **Date** _____

1. Look at each number in the table. Complete the missing numbers and write the rule for the table.

IN	4	5	6	7	8	9	10
OUT	24	30	36	42			
RULE:							

2. Look at each number in the table. Complete the missing numbers and write the rule for the table.

IN	108	99	90	81	72	63	54
OUT	12	11	10	9			
RULE:							

DAILY Warm-Up 41

Name _____ Date _____

1. Janet and Linda love sewing blankets. For every 3 blankets Janet sews, Linda sews 6. If Linda has sewn 48 blankets, how many blankets has Janet sewn?

Explain how to find the answer: _____

_____

_____

2. In which number sentence does 8 make the equation **true**? (*Circle the letter of the correct answer.*)

A. $56 \div 7 = \boxed{}$ **B.** $42 \div 7 = \boxed{}$ **C.** $36 \div 4 = \boxed{}$ **D.** $30 \div 6 = \boxed{}$

DAILY Warm-Up 42

Name _____ Date _____

1. Look at each number in the table. Complete the missing numbers and write the rule for the table.

IN	6	7	8	9	10	11	12
OUT	36	42	48	54			
RULE:							

2. Which figure would come next in the following pattern? (*Circle the letter of the correct figure.*)

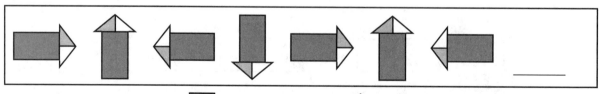

A.   **B.**   **C.**   **D.**

Name _____ Date _____

Warm-Up 43

1. What is the next figure in this pattern? (*Circle the letter of the correct figure.*)

A.   B.   C.   D.

2. In which answer choice does the number 7 make all the equations **TRUE**? (*Circle the letter of the correct choice.*)

A.	B.	C.	D.
56 ÷ 8 = ☐	56 ÷ 8 = ☐	56 ÷ 7 = ☐	14 ÷ 7 = ☐
14 ÷ 2 = ☐	63 ÷ 9 = ☐	21 ÷ 3 = ☐	56 ÷ 7 = ☐
21 ÷ 7 = ☐	28 ÷ 4 = ☐	42 ÷ 6 = ☐	35 ÷ 5 = ☐
40 ÷ 5 = ☐	7 ÷ 1 = ☐	63 ÷ 9 = ☐	7 ÷ 1 = ☐

Name _____ Date _____

Warm-Up 44

1. Write the fact families for the numbers 4, 6, and 24.

_____ x _____ = _____   _____ ÷ _____ = _____

_____ x _____ = _____   _____ ÷ _____ = _____

2. Which answer choice is an example of a **reflection** of the arrow below? (*Circle the letter of the correct answer.*)

   A.

    B.

    C.

    D.

Name _____   **Date** _____

DAILY
Warm-Up 45

1. Look at the function machine. If the "IN" number is 3, what will be the "OUT" number? (*Write the number on the line.*)

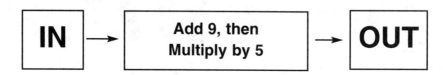

| IN | → | Add 9, then Multiply by 5 | → | OUT |

The "OUT" number will be _____.

2. In which answer choice does the number 5 make all the equations true? (*Circle the letter of the correct choice.*)

A.	B.	C.	D.
$30 \div 6 = \square$	$40 \div 8 = \square$	$35 \div 7 = \square$	$10 \div 2 = \square$
$10 \div 2 = \square$	$45 \div 9 = \square$	$30 \div 6 = \square$	$30 \div 5 = \square$
$25 \div 5 = \square$	$35 \div 7 = \square$	$45 \div 9 = \square$	$35 \div 7 = \square$
$40 \div 5 = \square$	$8 \div 1 = \square$	$20 \div 4 = \square$	$5 \div 1 = \square$

- -

Name _____   **Date** _____

DAILY
Warm-Up 46

1. Look at the function machine. If the "IN" number is 5, what will be the "OUT" number? (*Write your answer on the line.*)

| IN | → | Multiply 6 then Divide by 3 | → | OUT |

The "OUT" number will be _____.

2. Write the fact families for the numbers 3, 7, and 21.

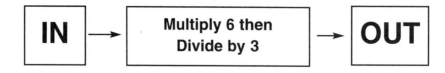

_____ X _____ = _____   _____ ÷ _____ = _____

_____ X _____ = _____   _____ ÷ _____ = _____

Warm-Up 47

1. Cindy made necklaces using different amounts of beads. She made a table of her results. If the pattern of beads used continues, how many beads will Cindy use if she makes five necklaces? (*Fill in the answer on the chart.*)

Number of Necklaces	Number of Beads
2	36
3	54
4	72
5	

2. Look at the figures below. If the pattern of cubes continues, how many cubes will be in the next pattern? (*Circle the letter of the correct answer.*)

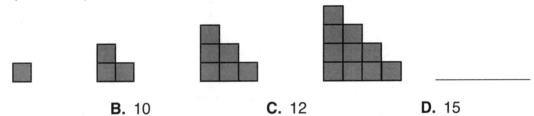

A. 8   **B.** 10   **C.** 12   **D.** 15

Warm-Up 48

1. Mrs. Kovar wrote the number pattern on the board. She explained the pattern and challenged her students to continue the pattern to find the next three numbers. If her class did this correctly, what were the numbers they gave? (*Fill in the answers on the lines.*)

6, 12, 19, 27, 36, _____, _____, _____

2. Look at the pattern of shapes. Draw the next figure in the pattern.

1. On Monday, Margaret rode her bike 2 miles. Every day she rode her bike twice as many miles as she did the day before. If this pattern continues, how many miles will Margaret ride her bike on Friday? (*Show your work. Write the final answer on the line.*)

_____

2. Sue bakes 4 pies each month. How many months will it take for Sue to bake a total of 36 pies? (*Show your work. Write the final answer on the line.*)

_____

---

1. Hannah loves to sew blankets. Every 4 days, she completes 2 blankets. How many days will it take for Hannah to sew 24 blankets? (*Show your work. Write the final answer on the line.*)

_____

2. Coach Parson is keeping a log of the number of home runs his students hit. For every 12 home runs his students make, 2 students strike out. How many strikeouts can Coach Parson expect if his students make a total of 60 home runs? (*Show your work. Write the final answer on the line.*)

_____

DAILY Name _____ **Date** _____

Warm-Up 51

1. Brandi scored 8 points higher on her math test than Gordon. Brandi scored an 86 on the test. Which equation below could find Gordon's math grade? (*Circle the letter of the correct equation.*)

    A. $86 + y = 8$ **B.** $86 - 8 = y$ **C.** $y - 8 = 86$ **D.** $8 - y = 86$

2. On the line, write a number sentence that reads 2 times a number is equal to 3 less than 15.

_____

- -

DAILY Name _____ **Date** _____

Warm-Up 52

1. Look at the equation. Is the equation true?

24 > 6 x 4

    Explain how to get the answer: _____

_____

2. Write **TRUE** or **FALSE** for the equations.

FALSE	$2 + 5 > 9$	_____	$12 < 9 + 4$	_____	$36 \div 4 = 9 \times 4$
_____	$4 \times 6 > 6 \times 6$	_____	$6 + 6 = 2 \times 6$	_____	$8 > 2 + 2 + 2$
_____	$3 + 9 = 12$	_____	$9 + 9 = 3 \times 6$	_____	$9 \times 3 < 6 \times 6$
_____	$5 + 5 > 10$	_____	$21 \div 3 > 2 \times 7$	_____	$7 \times 4 > 12 + 9$

Name _____ **Date** _____

Warm-Up 53

1. What number belongs on the line? (*Circle the letter of the correct number.*)

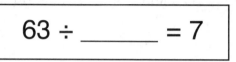

$$63 \div \underline{\qquad} = 7$$

A. 7 **B.** 8 **C.** 9 **D.** 10

2. Which pair of numbers best completes the equation? (*Circle the letter of the correct pair.*)

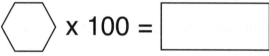

$x \ 100 =$

A. 345 AND 3,450 **C.** 34 AND 340

B. 345 AND 34,500 **D.** 345 AND 1,725

Name _____ **Date** _____

Warm-Up 54

1. The number 9 makes which of the following equations **FALSE**? (*Circle the letter of the correct equation.*)

A. $9 \times n = 36$ **B.** $3 \times n = 27$ **C.** $2 \times n = 18$ **D.** $5 \times n = 45$

2. Jason is practicing for a swimming contest. The table below shows the number of laps he swims each day. How many laps will Jason have swum after 9 days of practice? (*Fill in the answer on the chart.*)

Number of Days	Number of Laps
1	50
3	150
5	250
7	350
9	

1. What number belongs in the box? (*Circle the letter of the correct number.*)

$$56 \div \boxed{} = 8$$

A. 7   **B.** 8   **C.** 9   **D.** 10

2. Which pair of numbers does not complete the equation? (*Circle the letter of the correct pair.*)

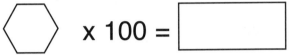

A. 〈124〉 AND [12,400]   **C.** 〈124〉 AND [1,240]

B. 〈12〉 AND [1,200]   **D.** 〈104〉 AND [10,400]

1. The number 5 makes which of the following equations **TRUE**? (*Circle the letter of the correct equation.*)

A. 9 x ____ = 36   **B.** 7 x ____ = 35   **C.** 8 x ____ = 32   **D.** 9 x ____ = 63

2. Which answer choice describes the table shown below? (*Circle the letter of the correct response.*)

A. The numbers in column Y are 3 less than the numbers in column Z.

B. The numbers in column Z are 3 more than the numbers in column Y.

C. The numbers in column Y are 3 times the numbers in column Z.

D. The numbers in column Y are 53 more than the numbers in column Z.

Y	Z
36	12
33	11
30	10
27	9
24	8

Name _____   Date _____

1. Jimmy owns a grocery store. To every 3,000th customer, he gives a $50 gift certificate. Based on the pattern, how much money in gift certificates will Jimmy give away if he has had 12,000 customers this month? (*Write the answer on the line.*)

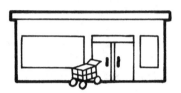

_____

2. Solve the problems below.

$84 \div$ ____ $= 12$ $63 \div$ ____ $= 9$ $48 \div$ ____ $= 8$

____ $\times 12 = 108$ $36 \div$ ____ $= 6$ ____ $\times 6 = 42$

$72 \div$ ____ $= 9$ $56 \div$ ____ $= 7$ $32 \div$ ____ $= 4$

Name _____   Date _____

1. What letters go next in the pattern below? (*Circle the letter of the correct pair.*)

| A, A, Z, B, B, Y, C, C, X, D, ____, ____ |

A. D and D   **B.** D and E   **C.** E and F   **D.** D and W

2. Lynn loves painting pictures using different colors of glitter. The table shows the number of bottles of glitter she uses for each picture. If the pattern continues, how many pictures can Lynn paint if she uses 7 bottles of glitter? (*Write the answer on the line.*)

Number of Bottles	Number of Pictures
2	16
4	32
5	40
8	64
10	80
12	96

_____

Name _____ **Date** _____

1. Look at the pattern of shapes. If the pattern continues, what would be the next two shapes? (*Circle the letter of the correct pair of shapes.*)

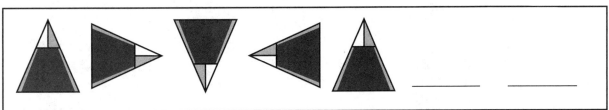

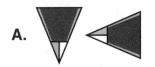 **A.**  **B.** 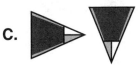 **C.** 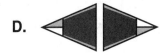 **D.**

2. Solve the problems below.

$(7 \times 4) + 5 =$ _____ $(9 \times 6) + 3 =$ _____

$12 - (21 \div 7) =$ _____ $14 + (14 \div 7) =$ _____

Name _____ **Date** _____

1. The table below shows the number of pages 4 friends read in a group reading contest in their class. Each friend, except Pete, wrote down the number of pages he read in the table below. They know that altogether they read a total of 450 pages. How many pages did Pete read? (*Write the answer on the chart.*)

Number of Pages Read	110	150		118
Name	Lou	Jim	Pete	Sam

2. The table shows the cost of apples. If Mary buys two apples, how much money will she spend? (*Write the answer on the line.*)

Number of Apples	Cost
1	$0.25
3	$0.75
5	$1.25
7	$1.75

_____

DAILY **Warm-Up 61**

Name _____ **Date** _____

1. Which number sentence is in the same fact family as 48 ÷ 6 = 8? (*Circle the letter of the correct response.*)

   A. 8 + _____ = 48   **B.** _____ − 8 = 48   **C.** 8 x _____ = 48   **D.** 54 ÷ 6 = _____

2. In which number sentence does 9 make the equation **TRUE**? (*Circle the letter of the correct response.*)

   A. 40 ÷ 4 = ☐   **B.** 36 ÷ 4 = ☐   **C.** 20 ÷ 4 = ☐   **D.** 45 ÷ 9 = ☐

DAILY **Warm-Up 62**

Name _____ **Date** _____

1. Look at each number in the table. Complete the missing numbers and write the rule for the table.

IN	5	6	7	8	9	10	11
OUT	40	48	56	64			
RULE:							

2. Look at each number in the table. Complete the missing numbers and write the rule for the table.

IN	96	88	80	72	64	56	48
OUT	12	11	10	9			
RULE:							

Answer Key

Warm-Up 1
1. 294 miles
2. C

Warm-Up 2
1. 65 miles
2. B

Warm-Up 3
1. B
2. It is multiplied by 4.

Warm-Up 4
1. $140
2. C

Warm-Up 5
1. 40 cans
2. 56

Warm-Up 6
1. C
2. C

Warm-Up 7
1. A
2. 26, 34, 43, 53

Warm-Up 8
1. D
2. 28

Warm-Up 9
1. $y = 4{,}389$
2. C

Warm-Up 10
1. 70, 84, 98
2. 150 customers

Warm-Up 11
1. 8 days
2. 18, 7, 8

Warm-Up 12
1. 36, 41, 45
2. $y = 2{,}458$

Warm-Up 13
1. B
2. B

Warm-Up 14
1. B
2. 14 blue buttons

Warm-Up 15
1. C
2. 48

Warm-Up 16
1. C
2. 15

Warm-Up 17
1. 20 times
2. C

Warm-Up 18
1. 16, 22, 29, 37
2. A

Warm-Up 19
1. C
2. 10 months

Warm-Up 20
1. 7 times
2. 10 shots

Warm-Up 21
1. C
2. C

Warm-Up 22
1. For each "IN" number, 8 is added to get the "OUT" number.
2. C

Warm-Up 23
1.

Name	Logan	Tanya	Harold	Rebecca
Number of Eggs	16	24	13	21

2. D

Warm-Up 24
1. 16 chocolate cupcakes
2. B

Warm-Up 25
1. 28 arrows
2. A

Warm-Up 26
1. 8 laps
2. D

Warm-Up 27
1. B
2. $3 \times \boxed{9} = 27$ $27 \div \boxed{3} = 9$
   $9 \times \boxed{3} = 27$ $27 \div \boxed{9} = 3$

Warm-Up 28
1. You would multiply 7 x 4 to get the number of candy bars in 7 boxes.
2. B

Warm-Up 29
1. B
2. 16

Warm-Up 30
1. 20 crayons
2. $6 \times 4 = 24$ $24 \div 4 = 6$
   $4 \times 6 = 24$ $24 \div 6 = 4$

Warm-Up 31
1. 10,000 points
2.

9	6	5
5	9	6
9	6	7

Warm-Up 32
1. B
2. 56

Warm-Up 33
1. C
2.

2	8	7
6	6	15
15	3	45

Warm-Up 34
1. Top to Bottom: orange, yellow, green, white
2.

7	2	2
24	9	6
27	21	15

Warm-Up 35
1. 11 pounds
2. IN: 5   OUT: 7
   The number 2 is added to each "IN" number to get the "OUT" number.

Warm-Up 36
1. D
2. 6 combinations

Warm-Up 37
1.

2. 30 cents or $0.30

Warm-Up 38
1. 63
2. 22   51
   7   17

Warm-Up 39
1. C
2. C

Warm-Up 40
1.

IN	4	5	6	7	8	9	10
OUT	24	30	36	42	48	54	60

RULE: Multiply by 6.

2.

IN	108	99	90	81	72	63	54
OUT	12	11	10	9	8	7	6

RULE: Divide by 9.

Warm-Up 41
1. Divide 48 by 2 to get the number of blankets that Janet sewed. (24)
2. A

Warm-Up 42
1.

IN	6	7	8	9	10	11	12
OUT	36	42	48	54	60	66	72

RULE: Multiply by 6.

2. B

Warm-Up 43
1. D
2. B

Warm-Up 44
1. 6 x 4 = 24   24 ÷ 6 = 4
   4 x 6 = 24   24 ÷ 4 = 6
2. B

Warm-Up 45
1. 60
2. C

Warm-Up 46
1. 10
2. 7 x 3 = 21   21 ÷ 7 = 3
   3 x 7 = 21   21 ÷ 3 = 7

Warm-Up 47
1. 90
2. D

Warm-Up 48
1. 46, 57, 69
2. ⬅

Warm-Up 49
1. 32 miles
2. 9 months

Warm-Up 50
1. 48 days
2. 10 strikeouts

Warm-Up 51
1. B
2. $2x = 15 - 3$

Warm-Up 52
1. The equation is not true because, although 24 equals 24, the equation states that 24 is larger than 24.
2. False   True   False
   False   True   True
   True   True   True
   False   False   True

Warm-Up 53
1. C
2. B

Warm-Up 54
1. A
2. 450

Warm-Up 55
1. A
2. C

Warm-Up 56
1. B
2. C

Warm-Up 57
1. $200.00
2. 7   7   6
   9   6   7
   8   8   8

Warm-Up 58
1. D
2. 56 pictures

Warm-Up 59
1. C
2. 33   57
   9   16

Warm-Up 60
1. 72
2. 50 cents or $0.50

Warm-Up 61
1. C
2. B

Warm-Up 62
1.

IN	5	6	7	8	9	10	11
OUT	40	48	56	64	72	80	88

RULE: Multiply by 8.

2.

IN	96	88	80	72	64	56	48
OUT	12	11	10	9	8	7	6

RULE: Divide by 8.